Simla

A HILL STATION IN BRITISH INDIA

Pat Barr & Ray Desmond

The Scolar Press · London

First published in Great Britain 1978 by
The Scolar Press Limited, 39 Great Russell Street, London WC1B 3PH
Reprinted 1979
Copyright © Pat Barr and Ray Desmond, 1978

ISBN 0 85967 405 3

The majority of the illustrations in this book are reproduced by permission of the
Director of the India Office Library and Records, whence they were obtained. Some
subjects however have other sources and the Publishers gratefully acknowledge the
help of the following in giving access to their records, supplying photographs, and
granting permission for material in their possession to be reproduced:
Radio Times Hulton Picture Library (pages 22, 41, 44, 99a); the Mansell
Collection (70, 77); Liddell Hart Centre for Military Archives, King's
College, London (65, 78, 92); Bindra Studios and the collection of
Judith M. Gutman (105); the National Army Museum (18); the collection of
A. M. Drummond (10); the collection of Terence Pepper (35).

Printed in England by The Scolar Press Limited, Ilkley, Yorkshire LS29 8JP

Frontispiece
Barnes Court, named after General Sir Edward Barnes, was the official residence of
the Commander-in-Chief in India from 1849 to 1865. It was one of the oldest of the
large Simla estates. With their matured gardens and roofs of slate or tile replacing the
earlier corrugated tin, such properties acquired considerable charm.

Contents

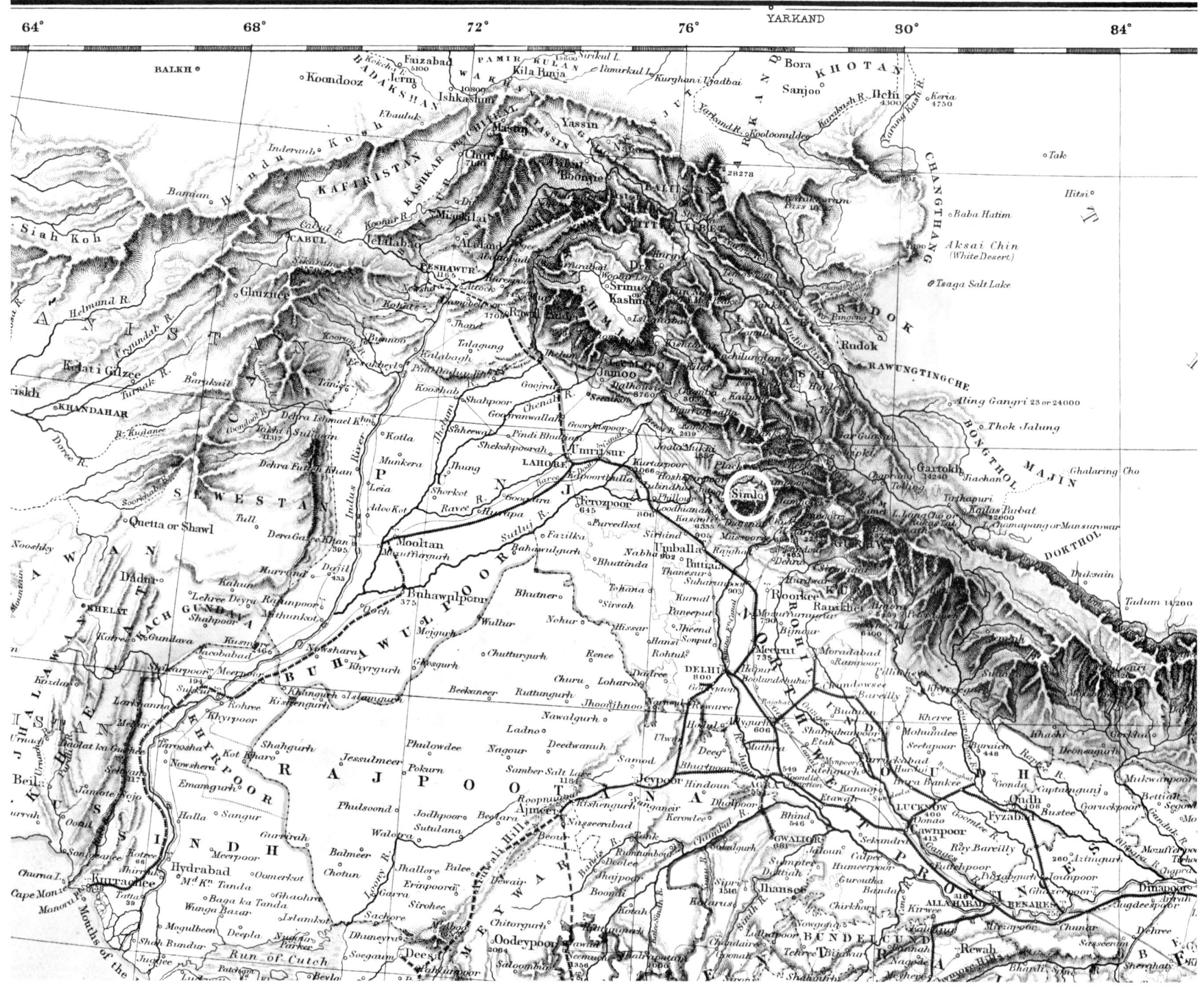

Section of a map of India, prepared by the Surveyor-General's office, 1877, showing
Simla in the foothills of the Himalayas. Scale: one inch to 130 miles.

SIMLA: the story of a hill-station
Pat Barr

Simla was a familiar name to the British in nineteenth-century India: it was called Mount Olympus, the Viceroys' Shooting Box, the Indian Capua, the Abode of the Little Tin Gods. It was a dream of coolness in a very hot land; a hope of healthy rest from the burdens of imperial office; a haven of familiarity pinnacled above the alien dust of the plains; a solace for the wounded and the desolate, the ill and the bored; a promise of fun and flirtation; above all, a bitter-sweet memory of home – cuckoos and thrushes, pines in the mist, honeysuckle and roses in the rain.

Simla was always a little insubstantial, as dream-filled places are. In the early days when the storms came, paths, roofs and hill-side gardens were often washed quite away, and people sometimes tumbled over un-parapeted precipices. It was difficult to reach and challenging to build upon; climbing there took your breath away, as did the occasional stupendous sunset over the distant snowy ranges of the Himalayas. The tonic of its clean, high, sharp air was irresistible. As time went by, more and more Anglo-Indians went there every year, arriving ever earlier in the spring and lingering ever later in the autumn – when the climate was at its most delectable and inspiriting.

The majority of Simla's European population was securely entrenched in the government and military hierarchies of British India; yet, perched on that 7,000 foot spur of the lower Himalayas, they were frequently assailed by the sheer audacity, absurdity, improbability of their ruling presence. As Miss Emily Eden, sister of Governor-General Lord Auckland, put it with her usual pith after the holding of the Queen's Ball of the 1839 Simla season:

Twenty years ago no European had ever been here, and there we were, with the band playing the 'Puritani' and 'Masaniello', and eating salmon from Scotland, and sardines from the Mediterranean, and observing that the chef's *potage à la julienne* was perhaps better than his other soups . . . and all this in the face of those high hills, some of which have remained untrodden since the Creation, and we 105 Europeans being surrounded by at least 3,000 mountaineers, who, wrapped up in their hill-blankets, looked on at what we call our polite amusements, and bowed to the ground if a European came near them. I sometimes wonder they do not cut all our heads off and say nothing more about it.

In fact, the time for a quiet and easy massacre of the foreign invaders was already past, as Emily Eden was comfortably aware – though had the hill-folk been sufficiently alert and decapitated the first British intruders on their mountain fastnesses, they might have kept the alien strains of *I Puritani* at bay for a while longer. But they made no such attempt, for, as the *Imperial Gazetteer* of 1887 reassures: 'All classes of the hill population in the Simla district have always been simple-minded, orderly people, truthful in character and submissive to authority, so that they scarcely require to be ruled.'

The first foreigner sent to impose rule over them was one Captain Charles Pratt Kennedy who, in 1822, was appointed Superintendent of the Hill States, with instructions to receive tribute from the hill chiefs and establish some rudimentary British-style law and order among them. The region had first come to the attention of the British during their wars against the Gurkhas (1815–16), after which a few officers were sent there on surveying expeditions, one of whom described Simla as 'A middle-sized village where a fakir is situated to give water to travellers.' But to Captain Kennedy is generally credited the building of the first permanent European-style house – knocked up in about a month by a hundred or so hillmen who felled and rough-hewed the timber on the spot to create a comfortable and 'spacious dwelling', according to a Frenchman, Victor Jacquemont, who stayed there in 1830.

Kennedy set the future tone of the place, for he was, according to Jacquemont, 'The first of all artillery captains in the world', an amiable, hospitable fellow who treated his guests to 'elegant and recherché breakfasts', 'magnificent dinners' that began at seven pm and ended at eleven, and plenty of inspiriting beverages. Already a sense of incongruity flickers across the visitor's mind: 'Do you see Simla on your map?' Jacquemont wrote to his father in Paris. 'A little to the north of the 31st parallel of latitude and a little to the east of the 77th meridian of longitude, a few leagues from the Sutlej? Isn't it strange to dine in silk stockings in such a place, to drink a bottle of hock and another of champagne each evening, to have delicious Moccha coffee and receive the

Calcutta papers every morning?'

Three years prior to Jacquemont's arrival, Lord Amherst had put Simla on the Anglo-Indian social map by being the first Governor-General to stay there. It was just possible to accommodate him, his immediate entourage and the baggage that a thousand coolies had dragged up the mountain, inside several wooden bungalows which had been built in the neighbourhood by other military gentlemen with a taste for the picturesque and unpopulated frontiers. However, the bungalows were 'not furnished better than a labourer's cottage in England,' according to Captain Raleigh, a junior on Amherst's staff who had to live in a tent.

So it was all rather comfortless, though the land that the Amherst party saw was doomed never to be quite so pristine again.

To give any description of the magnificence of this scene would be out of my power [wrote Raleigh from his Simla perch]. Downwards and to your right hand, you looked over the vale formed by faces of the opposite mountains, the whole of which were clothed with wood of the most gorgeous description. The stately 'deodora', a large oak, and other majestic trees thickly interspersed with rhododendron trees as large as apple trees, in fruit and brilliant scarlet blossoms, giving an idea of looking over a gaudy carpet of scarlet and green.

Wild strawberries, raspberries, apricots and cherries (excellent for making brandy) ripened along the nearby hill paths, deer lurked among the pines, and when the aides-de-camp tired of playing cards round the log fires, they strolled through the woodlands taking potshots at any mountain bears, leopards or golden eagles which chanced their way.

In the following year, 1828, Lord Combermere became the first Commander-in-Chief of the Indian Army to arrive in Simla, and on his staff was one Captain Mundy who, while his chief was quartered in Kennedy's house, had to make do with 'a canopy of planks lined with whitewashed canvas' – and thus became the first of many Simla residents to complain bitterly of roofs that leaked most abominably during summer rainstorms. During his stay, Mundy records, Lord Combermere 'amused himself and benefited the public by superintending the formation of a fine, broad, level road round the Mount Jakko, about three miles in length.' Jakko was the highest peak near Simla, and Combermere's road became so well trodden that, in the view of a later visitor, 'The great event of every day is the Jakko promenade, which has almost a sacred and devotional character in honour of the god of the mountain.' In furtherance of pedestrian and equestrian convenience, Combermere also ordered the construction of a pinewood bridge, which was named after him, across the deep ravine that divided the two parts of the sprawling village.

A mere ten years separated the visits of Lords Combermere and Auckland but, during that interval, Simla had become a hill-station proper. It was acquired for the Government of India by Auckland's predecessor, Lord William Bentinck, who built a hill-top residence for himself there known as Bentinck's Castle. The station could boast two bazaars, a main thoroughfare which was called the Mall (though it was little more than a winding hill-track), and more than a hundred residences. Nearly all the residences had chimneys and snug fireplaces and were dubbed with cosy, home-like names such as Woodbine Cottage, Primrose Hill, Oakfield, The Hermitage and Sunnybank. Most of them were tenuously perched on the slopes of Mount Jakko, on the summit of which was a small shrine dedicated to Hanuman, the monkey god. Appropriately, troops of brown monkeys lived up there and, in later years, a holiday treat for the pallid Anglo-Indian children of Simla would be to climb up and feed biscuits to the lively creatures.

The houses were built of uncut stone walls and with flat roofs. According to an early resident, these roofs had a wooden base, and

A quantity of dried leaves is then thrown on the roof and on this again, earth, till the latter attains a thickness of three or four inches, when it is well beaten down by a man who sits on the roof pounding away for hours with a little wooden tool made for the purpose.

Notwithstanding all this effort, the roofs tended to melt into such insubstantial quagmires during the summer rains that, wrote Emily Eden, two of her brother's staff, quartered in especially leaky bungalows, had to dine with umbrellas held over their heads and their dinners.

The bazaars too had their shortcomings, being plentifully supplied with cheap, locally-grown produce and locally-made cloth, but seriously lacking in other practical necessities, as Emily and Fanny Eden discovered when they set about making a home there. They lived in Auckland House, which their brother had purchased, for Bentinck Castle had been taken over as the residence of the Commander-in-Chief. The house 'had been an immense labour to furnish properly,' Emily complained in a letter home. They had sufficient in the way of chandeliers and carpets, but 'We did not bring half chintz enough from Calcutta, and Simla grows rhododendrons and pines and violets, but nothing else – no damask, no curtain rings, no glazed cotton for lining, nothing. . . .'

Yet never mind all that, Emily decided, for the hills possessed the greatest of all blessings in India which was air that could actually be breathed. Arriving at Simla, 'I remember all about it,' she wrote. 'It is a cool sort of stuff, refreshing, sweet and apparently pleasant to the lungs.' And Auckland House itself was 'a jewel' – cosy, one-storeyed, with log-fires blazing in every room, and Emily got hold of a 'native painter', and 'cut out patterns in paper which he then paints in borders all round the windows and doors' to make up for the want of cornices and the 'eternal

Lithograph of the view of Simla from Colonel Chadwick's house at Mahasu.
'It is impossible to describe the delicious feeling of awaking at Simla for the first time, and looking out upon the purple and shadowy dells below, and the dark dense woods around, and the spotless Himalayas in the distance, and the moss and ivy on the trunks on the oak and pines about your path, and the dewy *English* wild flower and fern underfoot. The intensity . . . of such a moment can neither be described or forgotten.' (G. P. Thomas, *Views of Simla*, London 1846).

9

white walls'. So, 'Altogether it is very like a cheerful, middle-sized English country-house and extremely enjoyable'. The dwelling stood on a small spur which, 'as a delicate compliment to the Eden sisters', as later guidebooks explained, was soon called Elysium, and its windows afforded splendid views of april-green valleys, distant snowy ranges and masses of those wild, red, forty-feet-high rhododendron trees.

In short, Simla was, in Miss Eden's considered opinion, the very first place in India that had been worth all the trouble of reaching. And that was no idle compliment, for in her day, and for many years afterwards, the station was by no means easy of access. The unpaved track up the mountain was a zigzag of hair-pin bends that skirted sickeningly along precipitous edges; it was subject to dangerous landslides and floodings during the rains, and was too narrow for even a four-wheeled cart. So travellers determined to get there had few options: the back of a hill-pony (usually chosen by able-bodied gentlemen who were warned to keep a wary eye out for mountain goats or monkeys who might leap across the track and frighten a skittish steed over the nearest cliff-edge) or a dhoolie, which was a wax-cloth and wicker litter used mainly by children and invalids, though its motion was once likened to 'sitting in a half-reefed top-sail in a storm'.

The alternative means of locomotion, the jampan, figures prominently in the earlier nineteenth-century accounts of Simla. It was a sort of sedan chair, fitted with curtains, strung on poles and carried by at least four bearers called jampanees. Ladies were usually carried up to the station in jampans and, once there, everyone used them frequently, for no wheeled carriages were allowed. But jampans were never popular; Emily Eden thought they were like 'upright coffins'. Certainly they were cramped and unsociable, their curtains leaked and flapped chillily, and jampanees adopted 'a peculiar shifting gait caused by wearing slippers too large for them' so that they were often out of step, causing the vehicle to lurch unpredictably.

Such trials must have been minor however compared to those of the wretched coolies who, in the absence of carts, carried most of the impedimenta for Simla's residents up the mountain on their heads and backs. Every year up to ten thousand males from the neighbouring hill-tribes were coerced into 'public service' for 'the conveyance of the baggage of government establishments, regiments and private parties'. The 'service' was badly paid and prevented the men from getting on with their own sowing and harvesting. But, 'This very morning,' recorded Miss Eden happily on 13 April 1839, 'a long file of coolies appeared, ascending the hill and the result was 25 boxes of *sorts* – preserves and sweetmeats and sardines and sauces from France, a box of silks and books

Emily Eden, by F. Rochard, 1835.

from ditto' and, greater than all these, needles, tapes, buttons and 'my two boxes of gowns and bonnets.'

All these items were quite indispensable to the conduct of normal life in the lower Himalayas, most especially the bonnets and silks, arrayed in which the two First Ladies of the Auckland entourage felt reasonably presentable to attend the increasing number of social entertainments that were 'got up' by the 'larking' young a-d-c's during the Simla seasons of 1838 and '39. There were twice-weekly band concerts on the terrace at Secretary's Lodge which offered lovely views over the Snowy Range, and those ladies whose husbands had been posted to Afghanistan went 'to console themselves with a little music and to take a little tea and coffee and talk a little.' Small 'en famille' dinners were arranged for the most companionable among them, 'when we can furnish gentlemen enough . . .' and there were even balls when the occasion warranted.

One such occasion was the arrival of Sikh envoys from the Punjab, come to pay their respects to Lord Auckland. When the ball was announced, Emily Eden was informed that the 'ladies of Simla had settled that they would not dance because they had no idea of dancing before natives'. 'Considering,' Miss Eden continued with some asperity, 'that we ask forty natives to every dance we give at Calcutta and that nobody ever cares, it was late to make any objection.' In the event, nearly all the leading ladies of Simla except three attended the ball and enjoyed themselves; as for the Sikhs, they, 'though poor ignorant creatures who are perfectly unconscious what a very superior article the Englishwoman is,' were all 'very quiet and well-behaved.'

Annandale really came into its own during the Edens' time. It was a green and pleasant valley near Simla, named either after a Dumfriesshire glen of the same name by some homesick Scotsman or, according to another story, after 'the first lady who graced its solitude', who was called Anna. The valley was shaded by pines, firs and the giant deodar cedars that sometimes grew to a height of 150 feet; 'matchless monarchs of the forest' as they were inevitably called. It was popular because it ideally suited the Victorian taste for romantic pastoral, the perfect backdrop for picnic luncheons, lovers' rendezvous, and *fêtes champêtres* where ladies and gentlemen held archery competitions, played battledore and shuttlecock and danced in the cool evenings to the strain of a fiddle.

The Fancy Fairs held at Annandale during the Aucklands' time were seasonal high-points. They began about ten o'clock and lasted for twelve hours or so and most of Simla's European population took an active part in the proceedings. For one of them, Miss Eden explains, 'A turnpike gate with a canvas cottage' was erected at the entrance, with a board announcing Charity Toll Bar, and one Captain P— dressed as a funny old woman collecting the dues. Through the gate were stalls a-flap with coloured bunting and selling 'a vast array of pretty commodities – all that silk, satin, lace embroidery with their manifold concomitants could produce,' according to an admiring gentleman visitor.

You could buy a dip in a lucky bag, or a painting done by the Honourable Emily herself, or have your fortune told by Captain C— disguised as a villainous-looking gypsy. You could partake of ham pasties and champagne in the marquee, and then for the fun of the pony races – with old Colonel F— wearing a natty satin jockey-jacket competing on his aged steed against fat Captain D—. And after dark there was a firework display and dancing on a boarded platform decorated with arches of flowers. All in all, it was not only the merriest fête imaginable, Emily Eden concluded, but raised sufficient funds for the opening of a 'native dispensary', to which the sick from the nearby hill-tribes and Tibetans soon came timidly over the mountains in hope of cure.

The natives were not, of course, the only ones who nourished such hopes when they came to Simla, for its health-giving attributes for Anglo-Indians were early proclaimed. Simla was a 'sanatorium', 'good for the liver' and 'good for the soul'; it shook 'the dreadful plains' dust out of a fellow's brain' and helped to preserve the constitution of those suffering from 'too much East', as the phrases went. As Miss Eden put it, 'Like meat, we keep better here.' Indeed, 'the sharp clear air is perfectly exhilarating. I have felt nothing like it – I mean nothing so *English* since I was on the terrace at Eastcombe.'

In the decade after the Eden sisters were allowed to return to the familiar purlieus of Eastcombe and Greenwich which they would rather never have left, increasing numbers of Anglo-Indian wives made it a practice to spend several months of every year in Simla, an arrangement which suited some much more than others. Honoria Lawrence, wife of the famous Henry, was there almost contemporaneously with the Edens, but led 'a very quiet life', as she told her husband. She was staying with a Mr and Mrs Baird and her description of their normal day was perhaps more typical of hill-station living than that of the ladies of Auckland House:

Well, he goes out of a morning to 'seek what he may devour', returns with a lot of pickles, preserves and dried fish; breakfasts heartily on them and other savoury messes, says he is suffering a great deal from Dyspepsia and goes out again. Comes in about two, eats a tiffin that would lay you or me up for a month; then lies down on the sofa and groans his old complaint is very troublesome. At sunset he goes out with Mrs Baird; dines at eight on every variety of mess, asks me for rhubarb and soda and inquires after my insides. Eating and grumbling are his chief employment.

Honoria, a fairly severe critic of others' behaviour, decided after a few weeks at Simla, that its usual conversation was 'a confused bundle of tinsel, rags and dirt – the contents of a dustpan, a many-sided buzz of scandal and vanity, hasty censure, mutilated praise and insincere profession', and longed only to rejoin Henry Lawrence on the plains the moment her health improved.

Other, less earnest wives apparently used Simla's vaunted health-giving properties to cover a multitude of sins – at least according to *The Delhi Sketch Book*, which was a sort of Indian *Punch*. One of its satirical articles about why so many women *really* went to Simla every year listed among the typical residents:

Good motherly Mrs A—because her children's health requires it, and little flirtatious Mrs B—who had no children, because her own did. Mrs C—certainly lived at the dullest of out-stations and everybody knew its weather half-killed her. . . . Miss O— went up because she was Miss O—and did not wish to be so any longer . . . while Mrs L—was determined that her daughters should not be long in the plains, so took them up the first season.

The presence of so many ladies who were either temporarily 'un-attached' or were seeking permanent attachment accounted for Simla's popularity with bachelors and for its early-acquired reputation as a resort for philandering and frivolity – haunt of the pleasure-seeker and the match-maker, the cad, the card, the fortune-hunter and the flirt.

The customary time and place to make the acquaintance of all the eligible and socially-desirable people in residence was the early evenings, when everyone took to the Mall. Wrote one Doctor Hoffmeister, a physician travelling with Prince Waldemar of Prussia in 1845:

No-one ventures to make his appearance there who is not mounted on a handsome horse; or who cannot sport the whitest linen, the most stylish cut of coat or showy uniform and white kid gloves, for one must need make special toilet here in order to enjoy the open air. Every creature is on horseback; even the fair sex dash along on fine spirited Arab coursers; and many an English lady may be seen galloping down the street followed by a train of three or four elegantly equipped officers, while others of more sedate age are carried about in jampans.

Later in the evening, any chance encounter on the Mall could perhaps be pursued at one or other of the many evening parties and dances. Here a-d-c's in dashing tail-coats with light blue facings, gold buttons and velvet cuffs flirted discreetly in the verandahs, just out of sight of the small, green Gurkha sentinels, and, according to Dr Hoffmeister, 'a great many sprightly old ladies, loaded with perfect gardens of flowers rush about in the polkas with incredible zeal.' Before he left, Prince Waldemar was given a royal send-off, the Doctor records, with 'an exceedingly brilliant fête', held at Annandale. 'A large floor laid with cloth had been put up in the centre of the lawn before three spacious tents hung with elegant drapery. Dancing was carried on and a colla-

Simla in and out of season. From *The Delhi Sketch Book*, 1 February 1853.

Lady with a parasol being carried in a jampan along the Mall. Watercolour by H. A. Oldfield of the Indian Medical Service, 1848. A note by the artist declares 'the lady is no portrait; though she is ugly enough to be an heiress; but such people dont usually come to India.' The jampan, described by one sufferer as 'a jolting, back-aching abomination', was a sedan-chair fitted with curtains, slung on poles.

tion – so-called tiffin – was served in the middle of the tent. . . . The splendour of this fête has won a great and far-spread fame which, indeed, it well deserves,' Hoffmeister concluded.

With all this going on, Simla's summer population continued to grow. An hotel was started by a Frenchman, so the food was good, but the rooms leaked badly during the rains. A cricket ground was laid out at Annandale and its race-course was improved – and this not before time, for, a visitor commented, 'Rarely does a meeting pass without some serious accident, such as a rider rolling down a precipice, either with or without his horse, into the valley below'. For evening entertainment, a small, stuffy oil-lit theatre called the Gaiety had been opened in the lower bazaar as part of the first Assembly Rooms and here the station's amateur dramatic club put on very amateur farces.

A few pioneering foreign merchants opened shops just off the Mall – open-fronted, timbered premises with a small-town frontier look about them. The first of these on record belonged to Messrs Barrett & Co, and 'but for their endeavours and the example set by them, the lovers of the roast beef of Old England would have been deprived,' commented traveller Charles French. At first, French noted, the slaughter of the Hindu sacred cow was prohibited, 'on account of the prejudices of the natives, but now this rule is somewhat more honoured in its breach than in its observance.' From butchery, the enterprising Mr Barrett went on to open Simla's first billiard room and racquet court and to become a founder-member of the old Simla Bank, which was first mooted in 1845 at the end of a particularly convivial dinner-party.

The foundation stone for Simla's first permanent place of worship had been laid the previous year, and the ceremony was attended by the Governor-General Lord Hardinge, who presented a large mortar captured in the wars for casting into the first church bell – and that was the kind of dull detail conscientiously recorded in all the early guidebooks about Simla, when it was beginning to establish a sense of its own parochial history that was only marginally affected by the sweep of the more dramatic events which shaped the broader story of the British Raj.

Soon after Emily Eden left, the station was black with widows whose husbands had been massacred in the disastrous invasion of Afghanistan in 1841 and '42, for which Lord Auckland had been quite substantially responsible. Some of the survivors of the calamity ended up there too, among them Lady Florentia Sale, who wrote one of the most vivid accounts of the campaign. Her tales of blood and violence 'excited much sympathetic curiosity in our peaceful society,' wrote Henry Oldfield, a surgeon who was in joint medical charge at Simla in the later '40s. But he felt that the gallant Lady Sale,

THE GLORIOUS FUN WE HAD AT SIMLA---(SEASON '54)

No. I.—A LITTLE SCANDAL.

Old Gent.—I GIVE YOU MY WORD OF HONOR MISS JONES, I SAW THOMSON AND MRS. SMITH WALKING TOGETHER NOT FIVE MINUTES SINCE.
Chorus of Ladies. ——— Oh ! ————Oh !——————SHAMEFUL !
N. B.—*Party in the foreground thinks* HE *knows something about* THAT.

No. II.—SUCH A JOLLY BALL.

From *The Delhi Sketch Book*, 1 January 1855.

The Glorious fun we had at Simla.   (Season 51).

No. 4.   The Mall. (Hyde Park with the Chill Off).

though certainly a clever and amusing character is not remarkable for her delicacy. On the first visit I made to her she was suffering from gout and – without giving me any warning, she suddenly thrust her leg, bared up to the knee, on to the dining-table, remarking, 'Scuse me *cocking* my leg up so high.

This quite scandalised the young man, though, as a doctor, he must have seen similar sights before.

Six years after the Afghan affair and following the sporadic violence of the Sikh Wars, the Punjab came under direct British control, and a number of high-ranking officers, after many years' service in the East India Company's Bengal Army, chose to retire to the rose-bordered lawns of some comfortable Simla villa rather than brave the rather chill and alien homeland. There was also an influx of younger administrators sent to the Hills to recuperate from bouts of Punjabi Head, a common affliction among those who laboured too long and stressfully with the recalcitrant natives in too much heat and dust.

Lord Dalhousie, ruler of British India at this time, spent two seasons at Simla, but he and his wife were less enthusiastic about it than most. 'This place has been greatly over-rated in climate and everything else,' Dalhousie complained in a private letter home, for it did nothing to improve either his own or his wife's health. He suffered from nose-bleeds, 'an inscrutable lameness of the right foot' and 'the same cold as November last' was still his the following August. He also had the misfortune to fall down one of the treacherous *khuds*, the steep fall-offs that edged most of Simla's roads. The Lieutenant-Governor of the Punjab had a similar accident, and – how delighted the newspapers will be, Dalhousie commented. They will say, 'Oh this comes of Governor-Generals and Lieutenant-Governors going into the hills. If they had stayed in the plains they would not have fallen down a precipice, either of them.' For Dalhousie was well aware that he was not very popular in the Anglo-Indian community, and neither was his wife, whom 'the Simla ladies' considered to be snooty.

The Dalhousies did not take to Emily Eden's modest 'little jewel' of a house either. They stayed either at Strawberry Hill, a wooden-framed house reputedly as charming as its name, or they removed themselves entirely to a cottage at nearby Mahasu, 'on a site a thousand feet higher than Simla,' where 'The air is purer and cool so that we wear winter clothes, have a fire and sleep in blankets.' But, as Anglo-India's top couple, the Dalhousies were never allowed to stay there long.

We have had a terrible fortnight of festivities [Dalhousie wrote a friend in October 1851]. Balls without number, fancy fairs, plays, concerts, investitures – and every blank day filled up with a large dinner party. You may judge what this 'Hill Station'

Lithograph of the Fancy Fair at Annandale in 1839. The 'toll-bar of charity is made of canvas, . . . and the magpie and cage on the wall beside the window were *painted* for the occasion. Sam Weller is one of Lord Auckland's Aide-de-camps; Mr Pickwick is a portly doctor; the Dragoon and the Hussar are officers in the Sikh service of *that* day (one French, the other English); and it may be seen, in spite of her petticoats, that even our gipsy girl wears the breeches.' (G. P. Thomas, *Views of Simla*, London 1846).

The Marquis of Dalhousie, Governor-General of India 1848-56.

has grown to when I tell you that 460 invitations were issued for the last ball at Government House, and most of them came too.

Sir Charles Napier, who was in command of the Indian Army during part of Dalhousie's rule, felt that so much needless gallivanting was bad for the morale of his officers, and that they should stay put in the plains with the soldiers, who had no choice in the matter. So he ordered restrictions on their hill-station leave, a measure that was greatly resented and gave rise to several satirical poems in *The Delhi Sketch Book*. One, entitled 'The Hills', began with Napier's lamenting that:

Sad Fate compels me—I must go,
Though me the climate kills,
To Simla I must wend my way—
I do not like the Hills!
The offices are all up there,
Governor and Councils,
And I must go, though not from choice—
I do not like the Hills!

Choice or not, Napier spent the summer of 1849 at Simla's Barnes Court, a rambling residence built on a southern spur of Mount Jakko, with forty-two acres of ground. Barnes Court was one of the station's oldest large estates, dating from 1830 when part of the land was bought by one of those early military gentlemen on the scene. The spot remained a favourite with the Army and, between 1849 and 1865, was the summer residence of no less than six Commanders-in-Chief. First among them was Sir Edward Barnes, formerly the Duke of Wellington's Adjutant-General at Waterloo, who gave it its name when he bought it in 1832.

Soon after his stay in Simla, Napier quarrelled violently with Lord Dalhousie and eventually resigned, which did not much concern the Governor-General, who had fractious relations with many of his Anglo-Indian colleagues. He was a political autocrat, greedy to acquire as much territory as possible for the British, and he pursued his territorial ambitions with great efficiency and zeal during his eight-year term of office. His efforts culminated in the annexation of the province of Oudh early in 1856, just before he finally left India, a proud and widely-acclaimed public figure.

Within three months of Dalhousie's departure the Indian Mutiny broke out at Meerut, a large military station about thirty miles from Delhi where the first killings of English civilians by the rebel Indian sepoys occurred. When the news of the outbreak first reached Simla there was some panic among the non-combatant Anglo-Indian residents who needlessly feared that their 'faithful little green Gurkhas' would take up arms against them. And, in the ensuing months, dreadful stories of the massacre at Cawnpore and the long ordeal of the besieged garrison at Lucknow, the capital of Oudh where Sir Henry Lawrence was killed, shuddered in the air. But in Simla all remained tranquil and Lord William Hay, Deputy Commissioner for the region, later reported that 'the utmost decorum and good order' prevailed in the Hill States during the crisis, and he praised the 'loyalty' of the Indian servants and guards.

Inevitably, the Mutiny had a profound psychological effect on Simla's residents, as it did on all Anglo-Indians; but on the surface nothing much was changed. So it must have been difficult for the ladies drinking their customary tea in the shaded verandahs on quiet afternoons to fully comprehend that the body of poor little Miss P—, which had danced every quadrille with such gusto during the previous summer, had been hacked to pieces and thrown down the Cawnpore well, or that dashing young Captain W—, who had won the championship pony race at Annandale last September, had been slashed to pieces on his saddle during the storming of Delhi's Kashmir Gate.

As uneasy peace returned to the country, many survivors of the conflict, some of them wounded, arrived in Simla bringing first-hand accounts of the violence they had witnessed and the perils they had undergone. Among them was William Howard Russell, a famous correspondent of *The Times* who, with his friend, Captain Alison, ascended the mountains on 14 June 1859. And,

At a turn of the road, I catch sight of a conical hill, covered with a deluge of white bungalows, dominated by a church behind, and above which again rises a steep sugar-loaf of fir trees. 'That is Simla! There is Mount Jakko!' I replied with pleasure and thankfulness. To taste such pleasure, we must be sick, wounded, roasted and worn-out in the dreadful plains of India.

On arrival, Russell stayed first at 'a large and ostentatious building – called the Simla Club – in truth an hotel' which was packed full of officers in various stages of painful recuperation from their Mutiny ordeals. He soon found, rather to his surprise, that Simla society was as frothy and insouciant as ever in spite of the country's recent revolt, and the Club was one of its focal points. As darkness fell, lights gleamed from the Club's many windows and

Syces holding horses and jampanees sitting in groups by their masters' chairs, are clustering round the verandah. Servants are hurrying in to wait on the Sahibs, who have come to dinner from distant bungalows.

As the clatter of plates suggested the approach of food, diners 'in every style of Anglo-Indian costume are propping up the walls of the sitting

William Howard Russell.

Wounded officers at Simla. From Atkinson, *The Campaign in India*, 1859.

In 1845 Prince Waldemar of Prussia and his suite visited Simla and entertained the local community with a splendid fete champetre at Annandale. Shortly afterwards he was killed watching the battle of Ferozshar. Lithograph by A. E. Scott.

room waiting for the signal to fall in.' They included

Soldierless officers of ex-sepoy regiments, Queen's officers, civilians, doctors, invalids, unemployed brigadiers, convalescents from wounds or illness in the plains, and all the talk is of sporting, balls, promotions, exchanges, Europe and a little politics re-chauffed from the *Overland Mail*.

At the announcement of dinner, they all

file into a large room with a table well laid with flowers and plated epergnes round which there is a double file of the Club servants and of the domestics which each man has taken with him. The dinner, at all events, is plentiful enough, pastry and sweets being perhaps the best department. Conversation is loud and animated. Among Anglo-Indians the practice of drinking with each other has not yet died out and the servants are constantly running to and fro with their masters' compliments, bottles, and requests to take wine with you, which are generally given to the wrong person and produce much confusion and amusement.

Cheroots and wine circulate freely and

. . . the fun grows louder and faster. The brigadiers look uneasily or angrily over their cards at the disturbers, but do not interfere. There is a crash of glass and a great row at the end of the room and the Bacchanalians, rising with much exultation, seize 'Ginger Tubbs' in his chair and carry him round the room as a fitting ovation for his eminent performance of the last comic ballad, and settle down to 'hip, hip hoorah and one cheer more' till they are eligible for their beds or for a 'broiled bone' at old Brown's.

Russell, who was suffering considerable pain from a leg injury, soon tired of so much noisy bonhomie, and he and Captain Alison moved into The Priory, a verandahed bungalow on the slopes of Mount Jakko. It consisted of a

hall, to the left, dining-room, on the right, sitting-room, and each of these with a small suite of sleeping-rooms and one bathroom for each, and at the back a row of stone huts and dirty outhouses

which was typical of the middle-level Simla establishment. The rent for the season was £60 and, as was the hill-station custom, 'sets of plated ware, crockery, lamps etc' had to be rented separately. The two men found that 'an abundance of servants' were awaiting hire and,

We selected a long-bearded khansamah [butler], a chief of jampanees or chaise-porters, and woodcutters who were engaged to the number of ten, bheesties [water-carriers], dhobies [laundrymen], cooks etc

making a grand total of thirty staff.

Confined to his bed on the verandah for most of the day, Russell learned to take an invalid's pleasure in the small-scale life around him – perhaps a relief from the chaotic terrors he had recently witnessed.

Hoopoes flashed in the nearby trees, ravenous crows sat waiting on the outhouse roofs for the daily washing of the rice-pots, kites and buzzards hung below the clouds. Seeing his interest in the natural life around, and hoping to hasten his recovery (for Russell's journalistic fame was considerable), people sent him caged green parakeets, yellow buntings and a talkative minah from Nepal. He acquired a hill-monkey with wistful eyes, a tame and bold ram with curved horns, and two jet black mountain bears that lapped milk greedily with their long thin tongues. Such creatures were still fairly easy to capture in the neighbouring countryside, for its natural fauna had not yet completely retreated. Apes with white-fringed faces lurked on many a lawn's edge, and there were horrid stories of pet lap-dogs being chewed up by marauding hyenas and leopards if they ventured too far from home at night.

In July the rains came, and Russell, still immobilised, felt that the low, dense clouds had fallen into bed with him; they seemed to have settled in his very boots, and his dressing-table was dank with their dew. For the next few weeks it was very wet, as was usual for the time of year. The valleys shone green and fresh, the slopes of Jakko were enamelled with wild geraniums, hill anemones, columbines and pheasant's eye, and the effects of the high-banked clouds tinted with rays of occasional gold and pink light over the distant mountains were magical; but for those who lived where the clouds precipitated so much of their moisture, it was all very boring. The young, deprived of their outdoor amusements, arranged their rendezvous in the covered racquet courts near the Assembly Rooms; the more mature, expected to continue with their usual evening parties, often groaned as they buttoned themselves into large mackintosh capes and goloshes to be carried three miles or so in a jampan through the pouring rain – which was rather like being inside a leaking diving-bell, Russell thought.

But he seldom ventured forth, preferring to look down from his verandah at the passing hill-folk, who added an oriental spice to even the most suburban Simla road. They mostly wore homespun, grubby woollen tunics and trousers, and those from the further East had a distinctly Tartar look about them, with high cheekbones and slit eyes. Some of the women were adorned with gold and silver nose-rings and ornaments made from goatskins were plaited in their front hair. They were a source of some disapproval (or curiosity or pity) to the memsahibs, for polyandry was a common practice among them. Though the hill-folk were 'immoral' and dirty, they laughed and sang most disarmingly and were amazingly honest in their poverty. Moreover, they were specially welcome in summer when they brought honey, nuts, peaches and apricots from the drier lands beyond the Sutlej, and some brought grapes swaddled in cotton from Konawar – to those households that had paid a seasonal subscription for the twice-weekly 'grape run'.

The chiefs of the hill-tribes paid tribute to the greater chiefs who resided in Simla, and, early one morning, Russell was aroused by 'the sounds of wild music from the huge horns of the Raja of Basahir passing to visit Lord William Hay'. Drums, fifes and trumpets brayed loudly and the Raja travelled in dignity, 'held aloft on a sort of tray . . . borne by men and half-obscured by an enormous scarlet umbrella with a gold fringe held over his head'.

Such exotic intrusions were welcome to Russell who found the strutured formalities of Simla rather tedious. 'The social distinctions are by no means lost sight of in India,' Russell observed. 'On the contrary, they are perhaps more rigidly observed here than at home, and the smaller the society, the broader are the lines of demarcation.' Each man's status was entirely dependent on his rank in the public service, which was a kind of aristocracy; women were totally dependent on their husbands for their own social position; and neither wealth, wit nor desirable connections could guarantee an individual breaking through 'the sacred barrier which keeps the non-official world from the high society of the services.' In consequence, and 'At a place like Simla where there is an annual gathering of all sorts of people, it is desirable to take care whom you know'. There was no easy middle ground for informal communication, for Simla, Russell noted, already had 'its St James's and its St Giles', the latter 'constituted by tradespeople and by the Crannies or Kerannes who are writers in the various offices and often Eurasians.'

Interestingly, Emily Eden, writing in the previous decade, had been similarly amazed, and constrained, by the rigidity of Simla's social attitudes.

There was a lady yesterday in perfect ecstasies with the music [of the band]. I believe she was the wife of an indigo planter in the neighbourhood and I was rather longing to go and speak to her, as she probably had not met a countrywoman for many months; but then, you know, she might not have been his wife, or anybody's wife, or he might not be an indigo planter. In short . . . you know what a world it is – impossible to be too careful etc.

William Russell's severest censures of Simla society were reserved for those Anglo-Indian officers who talked about their servants as 'dogs of natives' and the many young gentlemen who 'are up here on leave and sick certificates' and whose 'wildness of spirit and lax notions of discipline and decency' were only too convincing a proof of Simla's 'miraculous health-restoring properties'. Russell opined that their excessive gambling, drinking and disorderly behaviour had a very bad influence on the local populace and that

Group of hill-folk, Simla.

a senior officer should be sent to all our hill-stations to exercise a proper, but not too rigid control over the fast invalids and riotous sick who recover themselves so boisterously.

Russell's own recovery was less enjoyable and for many weeks he continued to suffer from fevers, 'queer confusions' of the head, and swelling of the leg which puzzled and alarmed the station's surgeons. But eventually he pulled through, and left Simla without any great regrets, for though it could be a haven of security and peace for the weak and the timid, there was not enough of the real raw India about it even in those days for one of his hardy and questing temperament.

Lord Canning, the first Viceroy under the Crown after the Mutiny, paid a brief visit to Simla in 1860, but his wife found the 'beauty of this place very questionable; it is such a sea of hill-tops and the snowy mountains are so far off and the dryness makes it all look wintry'. Moreover, she soon tired of the sameness of the roads, 'always with what we call here a khud (a sort of rocky precipice of hillside hundreds of feet down, and a wall of the same above).' The most enjoyable part of Lady Canning's stay was the expedition she made from Simla to the interior as far as the River Sutlej which she crossed in a basket swung on ropes. She was accompanied by Lord William Hay, for, as she explained in a personal letter to Queen Victoria (whose lady-in-waiting she had formerly been), 'These places I had not a chance of seeing in my husband's company, as he must always be within reach of telegraph and rapid posts', a restriction that many Simla-based Heads of State found irksome.

In spite of such difficulties of communication and transportation, it was on the initiative of an 'old India hand' – Sir John Lawrence, younger brother of Sir Henry – that Simla became the official summer headquarters of the Government of India a few years later. John Lawrence was rather unexpectedly appointed Viceroy in 1863, following the sudden death of Lord Elgin. Then a man of late middle-age, with more than thirty years experience of the country, he was of the considered opinion that Calcutta was no fit place from which to carry on government throughout the year, and that it would be infinitely preferable to remove himself, his Executive Council and departmental staff to the hills every summer.

Of all the hill-stations [he wrote to the Secretary of State] Simla seems to me the best for the Supreme Government. *Here* you are with one foot, I may say, in the Punjab, and another in the north-west provinces. Here you are among a docile population and yet near enough to influence Oudh. Around you, in a word, are all the warlike races of India, all those on whose character and power our hold in India, exclusive of our

Sir John Lawrence, later Lord Lawrence, Viceroy of India 1863-9.

own countrymen, depends. . . . Nowadays you have no large native army to fear. What you have on this side of India, you have mainly around and about you, so that your Governor-General, if he has any discernment, is well placed to perceive the first signs of danger and is then able to apply a remedy.

A few years before, such a proposal would have presented insuperable difficulties of access, but by Lawrence's time, the long-planned cart-road from the plains, first mooted by Lord Dalhousie, was in operation. It was to be called The Great Hindustan and Tibet Road, and, that incorrigible expansionist had written in 1851, 'It will not be surpassed, I flatter myself, by any mountain road in the world. . . . My project is to extend it to the Chinese frontier about 140 miles further on, with the same gradients.' The entire route had not been completed fifteen years later, but, as far as it went, the new road was a great improvement on the older, narrower track – and cheap at the price, for it was mainly constructed by 'free labour' conscripted from the neighbouring tributary hill-states.

The sight of the Heads of State and their extensive entourages ascending the mountains by this road was indeed remarkable, according to a journalist, Andrew Wilson, who once beheld it. There were colonels and clerks of departments and other 'men so tremendous in their own spheres'; assistant deputy commissioners, still relatively unburdened with the cares of highest office, 'cantering lightly along parapetless roads skirting precipices'; the 'ton weight of a Post Office official requiring twenty groaning coolies to carry him'; an Anglo-Indian damsel tripping graciously into a traveller's bungalow for a short rest.

She was probably having a bumpy ride up in a tonga, which was a two-wheeled, covered cart of the curricle variety, drawn by a couple of ponies. For, now that the road was wide enough, tongas, open carts and waggons drawn by bullocks or horses were used to drag up to Simla all the secretariat files, imported delicacies and personal clothing for the residents. According to a contemporary guide to 'Indian Outfits', the amount of the last that a lady would require for a stay in the hills should include, at the very least, 'four loose morning wrappers, several afternoon dresses of silk or cashmere, two piqué riding habits, with dogskin gloves, two ball-gowns and good black silks for evening wear', evening cloak, goloshes, parasols, lace and ostrich feathers for trimmings as required.

Unfortunately the improved road did not mean that everyone and everything always arrived intact. Precious baggage was often 'pitchforked on to rickety bullock hackeries and shaken as only hackeries can shake goods and left to the mercy of rainstorms and avalanches of mud and stone from the mountainsides.' This happened so often, explained a local guidebook, which contained several advertisements of local stores, that Simla merchants were simply forced to charge high prices for their

wares in order to recoup some of their losses.

Discounting problems such as these, and the fact that Simla was 1,170 miles from the seat of Government at Calcutta, Sir John Lawrence continued to urge the summer move on the grounds that

The work of government is probably treble, possibly quadruple what it was twenty years ago, and it is, for the most part, of a very difficult nature. Neither your Governor-General nor his Council could really do it in the hot weather in Calcutta. At the very best they would work at half speed.

Also, as Lawrence freely confessed, he hoped the change would benefit him personally, for even his iron constitution had begun to falter and his doctors had warned him against too much hard work. Indeed, once the summer move to the hills was accomplished, the Simla ambience did persuade the Chief Executive to relax occasionally.

It was delightful to see Sir John Lawrence, with other high and mighty statesmen at the close of a laborious day, entering with the zest of boys into the intricacies of the laborious game,

wrote an official who had spent thirty-eight years on the Indian scene.

The game in question was croquet, which was all the rage in the 1860s. 'June 9th – a croquet match at Annandale,' wrote Jane Maria Strachey in her journal. She was the twenty-three-year-old wife of Richard Strachey, an administrator and scientific adviser to the Government, and, on that lovely summer day, she had three first-rate games – she and Captain Stewart against Nina Plowden (a relative of hers) and Captain Gray. The year was 1863 and the pace was fast and furious for those in the right circles. Jane Maria certainly was, for she was the daughter of a well-known senior official, Sir John Peter Grant, and she had been accustomed to Indian affairs since her birth – which had taken place in an East India Company ship while it was rounding the Cape of Good Hope in a violent gale.

The evening prior to the croquet match, Jane Maria had attended Simla's annual Bachelors' Ball. 'My dress, an invention of Nina's and mine, was a great success,' she wrote in her journal. 'It was black and white net, and my white lace flounce looped at the bottom. Colonel Tombs was quite struck with it.' In the course of a hectic evening, she 'beguiled Colonel Durand into dancing the Lancers,' and had 'an excellent galloppe with Captain Stewart.' Then, 'We had a cotillion; it was not very good; there were too many people who were not up to the spirit of it.' She was taken into supper by Captain Grant and afterwards danced with Colonel Torrens, 'who waltzes very well, but can't go beyond a certain time.' And lastly, 'The Burlesque struck up and I never heard such a pace as the Band played it at. They were tired and wanted to tire us,' which was understandable, as the clock struck 4 am just as they left – to go jogging home in jampans by the light of a cool Himalayan dawn.

The day after the croquet match there was a gathering at Barnes Court, with the fun of an Aunt Sally, a shooting match, billiards indoors and more croquet on the lawn. And the following week the Stracheys made up a select party to go to Fagoo, several miles into the hills. There they found

The most beautiful turfy slopes where we stayed all the rest of the day enjoying ourselves much. Richard sketched, I read *Lord Toppington* to the two Misses Norman and Nina drew the most admirable likeness of me in the act of so doing. We came home by a long and romantic path.

Sketching, incidentally, was a popular pastime among Anglo-Indian ladies, most of whom took their drawing materials to Simla in the hope of being especially inspired by the grandeur of the mountain scenery. Judging from those sketches that survive, it does not appear often to have been the case. Other female artists of more purposeful inclination used to specialise in flattering portraits of Simla's VIPs. A passing journalist once commented scathingly that one civilian's wife 'took the likenesses' of the then Viceroy 'in every possible attitude both on foot and on horseback in order to curry favour for her "sad fool" of a husband.' But Lady Jane Maria needed no such stratagems: her husband became a chief consulting engineer to the Government and a member of the Council, and she matured into a cultivated, lively-minded woman who lived long enough to number among her friends members of the Bloomsbury Group, whom she met through the eldest of her thirteen children – Lytton Strachey.

Back in 1863, when the world was still young for Jane Maria, Simla was maturing rapidly. Following its elevation as the official summer headquarters of the Indian Government, the station was soon similarly used by the Army and the Punjab Government. It was now indeed the 'Capua of India', the 'Indian Mount Olympus' where the 'heavenly borne' (i.e. the covenanted civilians of the Indian Civil Service) could be met at work and at play – and perhaps be suitably, if unobtrusively, impressed.

Wrote a visitor:

Simla differs from Mussoorie. It is so much more sedate. More than half of those who prefer Simla do so in the hope of prepossessing one or other of the great authorities by being brought into contact with them and thus obtain staff employment or promotion, and very amusing it is to look at the public entertainments and witness the feelings of jealousy and envy that swell the hearts of the various candidates for notice and favour.

It was a theme amusingly pursued by George Aberigh-Mackay, author of some satirical essays on Anglo-Indian social life entitled *Twenty-One Days in India*. After characterising the typical Political Agent as a dry, earnest and intellectual fellow, he adds that at Simla, however, he can be seen in a different role – 'Wooing that hoyden Promotion in her own sequestered bower. How simple he is! How boyish he can be and yet how intense! He will play leap-frog at Annandale; he will paddle about in the streams below the waterfalls without shoes and stockings. . . .' To sum up: Simla was supposed to be the original place where one couldn't get a good night's sleep due to the sound of grinding axes.

The amount of business connected with an increasingly complex administration certainly meant that most of the officials who had attained those much-envied high ranks were overworked and often over-strained into insomnia. But one of the few obvious signs of their behind-the-scenes bustle was the number of chaprassies (messengers) who importantly stalked the Simla streets clad in red Imperial liveries. It was their duty to carry the locked dispatch boxes containing official documents, usually in triplicate, from one office to another and they were, according to Aberigh-Mackay, 'the receivers-general of bribes' and the retailers of all the latest scandals. Simla's servants had a bad reputation generally for tale-bearing and dishonesty; nevertheless, as the place became more popular and prosperous, numbers of domestics chose to live there the whole year round, for their services were much in demand during the summer months. Some of the regular residents preferred to bring their own servants up with them, but 'plains-people' were notorious for coming down with inconvenient colds and fevers in the mountain airs and so were less use than the acclimatised, if untrustworthy, locals.

By the early '70s the station attracted numbers of Anglo-Indians who returned regularly every year; they usually stayed in the same houses, and a strong sense of local pride and loyalty had developed among them. The Simla municipality, created in 1850, was the oldest in the Punjab and its activities were effective – as chronicled in Edward J. Buck's *Simla Past and Present*, a loving and careful study of the station written by a man who spent most of his life there. As Buck points out, its history was already fairly long by Anglo-Indian standards: the oldest decipherable monument in its first cemetery was to Charles, infant son of one Captain Henry Garston of the 10th Regiment Light Cavalry who died there in July 1829; one of the better known was of Sir Alexander Lawrence, eldest son of Honoria who had been in Simla in Emily Eden's time, and who was killed when a bridge collapsed on the Great Hindustan Road along which he was riding; one of the most poignant recent additions commemorated the deaths of four young Italian musicians between the ages of thirteen and seventeen who were touring India giving concerts and were all killed when a large rock fell on the open bullock-cart in which they were travelling up to Simla.

The municipal officers, Buck explains, had the duty of keeping the cemeteries in good trim, of propping up and repairing the road edges and wooden bridges that had a continuing tendency to fall over hillsides, of enforcing regulations to limit the passage of wide bullock carts down narrow alleys and of ensuring that householders trimmed their hedges and cleared 'the jungle' from their own grounds. In the bazaars, drains and slaughter houses were now inspected daily, so that the much-vaunted clean air was purer than it had been.

Horse-dealers, grain merchants, sellers of fowls, livestock and spices came from afar to those bazaars and lodged in their ramshackle *serai*. Several firms from Calcutta had opened branches there as had 'wealthy Mussalmen' from Delhi and Lahore so that, in addition to the usual run of shops selling provisions, locally made furniture and cloth, there were hosiers and milliners, civil and military tailors, gunsmiths, haberdashers, saddlers, confectioners, watchmakers, wine merchants, perfumers, photographers. There was Hamilton's, the jewellers from Calcutta (established in the reign of George III) and Mrs O'Brien's butchery that specialised in daily meat deliveries to householders, and there was a grocers who advertised that they were 'Licensed to Retail Wonders', much to everyone's amusement.

One of the most fascinating of Simla's shops to which everyone went in search of curios was opened in 1871 by a man of uncertain origins who became quite a figure on the local scene. His name was A. M. Jacob, an art dealer, jeweller and collector of eastern antiquities, who was also reputed to be a mesmerist, a Russian spy, an astrologer and a conjurer. He later figured in two novels: as the hero of Francis Marion Crawford's *Mr Isaacs*, and as Lurgan Sahib in Rudyard Kipling's *Kim*. In the latter work his shop is described as crammed full of wonders:

ghost-daggers and prayer-wheels from Tibet; turquoise and raw amber necklaces; green jade bangles; curiously packed incense sticks in jars crusted over with raw garnets; the devil-masks of overnight and a wall full of peacock-blue draperies; gilt figures of Buddha and little portable lacquer altars; Russian samovars with turquoises on the lid; egg-shell china sets in quaint octagonal cane boxes; yellow ivory crucifixes – from Japan of all places.

Some of these treasures were undoubtedly brought to Jacob's shop by the 'long lines of camels and caravans of oxen carts that unceasingly for six months of every year pour into the bazaar the luxuries of Hindustan and the magnificent comforts of Europe' as witnessed by an anonymous contributor to *Chambers' Journal* of 1872.

Amid all her greatness however, Simla never forgets her origins but still, as of old, barters with the simple shepherds of Tibet. Wild and unkempt-looking fellows are these Tibetans with their long hair falling over their shoulders and their sheepskins and woollen jackets hanging down – men of rags and dirt.

The Tibetans rub dirty shoulders with the even more numerous Hindus who like nothing better than to squat smoking with a group of friends and

The bustle, closeness, smells, flies, pariah dogs and all the attractions of the bazaar are to them more pleasing than the majestic tranquility of mountain and valley and far-off plains.

Standing somewhat aloof from the exotic, thrilling delights of the bazaar – which was the only place in Simla that offered any sense of the 'real India' which held such an ambivalent allure for many Anglo-Indians – stood the Royal Hotel. It was the most central, prestigious establishment for short-stay European visitors. It offered fine views of the distant snowy peaks; it served breakfast at nine o'clock, tiffin at two pm and dinner at seven; it levied extra charges for kerosene lamps, wax candles, kettles of hot water and quarts of English porter. The two local newspapers then published, *The Himalayan Advertiser* and *The Simla Advertiser*, were always available in the 'comfortable and well-stocked lounge', and books could be borrowed from the Simla Library (which, according to one visitor, contained some six thousand novels, all of them 'lightweight reading matter for lightweight minds').

For those of more serious bent, there was the Simla museum, housed in a former boarding establishment called Bonnie Moon and having on display specimens of Indian flora and fauna, rare oriental manuscripts and the marriage settlement of the last King of Delhi. The museum had been founded by Colonel Robert Tytler, who had had an honourable career in the Company's service. He had fought in the Siege of Delhi, during which his wife Harriet, marooned in the army lines, produced the only known English baby to be born on the famous Delhi Ridge during that long weary summer of 1857. Both the Tytlers were early enthusiasts of the modern hobby of photography and received instruction in the art from Mr Beato. Their collection of calotype negatives showing scenes of post-Mutiny destruction at Delhi, Lucknow and Cawnpore were acclaimed by the Royal Photographic Society of Calcutta in 1859 and some were on display in the Simla Museum.

After their retirement to Simla, Harriet Tytler, an energetic and courageous woman, reflected the growing interest in philanthropic activity that characterised later Victorian times by opening an 'Asiatic Christian Orphanage' for Eurasian and Indian girls. There, according to W. Carey's *Guide to Simla*, the poor children could be 'rescued from ignorance and neglect' and were taught useful trades, while not being 'raised above their natural position in life'. Boys of more elevated circumstances could attend the Bishop Cotton School, named after a Bishop of Calcutta who had been at Rugby under Doctor Arnold, and there were one or two select institutions for girls. One of them was in Auckland House, which had sadly dwindled from its earlier status of being a Governor-General's residence into a boarding-house, and then became a girls' school where females of good background could 'learn the rudiments of the three R's, embroidery and the pianoforte'.

'The prevailing tone of Simla society', wrote Andrew Wilson, 'is set by the Viceroy and his lady.' And the tone created by the Lords Mayo and Northbrook who succeeded Lord Lawrence was one of worthy diligence and earnest endeavour that did not add much colour or gaiety to the life of the station. So it was Lord and Lady Lytton, who first went to Simla in 1876, who were considered to be the first truly stylish and fashionable pair to inhabit Peterhoff, then the official government residence.

The first Viceroy to live there had been Lord Elgin in 1863, and it had reasonably served the requirements of several others, who took the view that the house, though not perfect, would last out their time. But, compared to other stately places Lord Lytton had known, he thought Simla 'a mere bivouac' and the viceregal residence 'a sort of pigsty'. Certainly it had a corrugated tin roof, as did most of the houses of the period, and, like most, it leaked chronically so that 'large pieces of plaster often used to come down from the ceiling,' according to Lady Lytton. Worse, there were only five bedrooms, so that guests had to sleep in adjoining bungalows and servants slumbered on mats in the passageways.

So much attentive proximity greatly oppressed Lord Lytton, who complained in a private letter that the most trying part of his existence was

that I cannot be for a second alone. I sit in the privatest corner of my private room and if I look through the window, there are two sentinels standing guard over me. If I go up and down stairs, an a-d-c and three unpronounceable beings in white and red night-gowns with dark faces run after me. If I steal out of the house by the back door, I look round and find myself stealthily followed by a tail of fifteen persons.

Nor was the sparkle of Simla society sufficient compensation.

Our own social surroundings are so grievously good [he wrote to Lady Salisbury]. Members of the Council and Heads of Departments hold prayer meetings at each other's houses thrice a week and pass the remainder of their time in writing spiteful minutes against each other. The young ladies are not allowed to dance lest they should dance to perdition; and I believe that moonlight picnics were forbidden last year by order of the Governor-General in Council lest they should lead to immorality. I wish I could report that our Empire is as well defended as our piety.

Lord Lytton, Viceroy of India 1876-80.

However, once settled, or rather crammed, into Peterhoff, the Lyttons set about doing what they could to lighten the stuffy social atmosphere. Lytton apparently quite shocked his staid Council Members by calling on their wives and holding levees in the evenings instead of during the day. 'But I fear I shall have to shock all the official proprieties more severely ere long,' he added cheerfully. The Lyttons had brought up from Calcutta a French chef, an Italian confectioner and about three hundred servants so Government House cuisine and service vastly improved. And the quantity of beverages consumed rather increased – to judge by those records of Peterhoff hospitality that still exist. On 11 October 1877, for example, there were fourteen guests to tiffin and thirteen to dinner. They drank between them six bottles of champagne, eight of claret, two of sherry, two of German beer, three of brandy, two of whisky; their personal servants accounted for four more clarets, three beers, four pints of porter and six glasses of brandy.

Lady Lytton enjoyed giving evening balls at Peterhoff, even though it meant turning the house upside down and removing doors from their hinges to accommodate the dancers. Lord Lytton was an enthusiastic theatre-goer and, during his period of office, Simla amateur dramatics were given a considerable fillip. The station's Gaiety Theatre had been opened in 1838 and boasted of having the first curtain in the Himalayas to be raised above a proscenium arch.

Performances in those distant days must have been rather dreadful, partly because it was still forbidden to ladies to tread the boards.

We had to go to another play last night [wrote Emily Eden in a letter home]. Luckily they only acted two farces so we were home at ten, but anything worse I never saw. There were three women's parts in the last farce and the clerks had made their bonnets out of their broad straw hats tied on; they had gowns with no plaits in them and no petticoats nor bustles. One of them, a very black half-caste, stood presenting his enormous flat back to the audience and the lover observed with great pathos, 'Upon my soul! that is a most interesting looking little gurl. . . .'

Forty years on conventions had relaxed and in every Anglo-Indian station 'the ladies' were as keen on performing as their menfolk. To encourage their efforts in Simla, Lord Lytton had the whole theatre redecorated and three new gilded boxes built – for the Viceroy himself, for the Commander-in-Chief and for the Lieutenant-Governor of the Punjab. Lytton also fancied himself as a producer and it was maliciously said of him that he used to recline on a gilded sofa in front of the stage to direct proceedings with a nonchalant wave of the hand. One season began with a production of Bulwer-Lytton's drama *Walpole*. It was a cumbrous play, creaking with Alexandrine verse which the players had much trouble in committing to memory, but as the Viceroy's father was its author, the effort was considered worthwhile.

Another Gaiety season opened with a production of a play called *Contrabandista*, and the libretto for it was written by Val Prinsep, the son of a well-known Indian administrator who took to art instead of government, and who had been commissioned to execute a painting of the Imperial Assemblage in Delhi in 1877, when Queen Victoria assumed the title of Empress of India. When Prinsep arrived in Simla, his first impression was of its 'unpicturesque' quality, like

an English watering place gone mad. . . . The world of Simla jogs or rather pushes along at its usual pace. All are bent on enjoying themselves and the champagne flows on every side. Every evening at eight, the roads are full of jampans conveying the fair sex to their festivities.

As a visiting artist Prinsep soon discovered that he had no recognised status in this close-knit, hill-station society that was structured solely on civil service and military hierarchies. Lacking many personal introductions, he therefore reached the conclusion that, in Simla,

Real sociability does not exist. . . . People pair off directly they arrive at a party as a matter of course, and the pairs, happy in their own conversation, do not trouble themselves about the general hilarity.

So poor Prinsep, though obviously a cultured and amusing man, was 'frequently left out in the cold.'

But the artist was on pleasantly familiar terms with the Lyttons. He enjoyed their cosmopolitan style and he painted a picture of them with their eldest daughter. It had been eight months since he had painted a white face instead of the brown and turbanned rajas and he found the difference 'quite odd'. He also admired the indefatigable industry with which the Viceroy performed his onerous task. 'He certainly hasn't an iron constitution,' Prinsep remarked, 'but he stands more work than most people. . . . He writes day and night and even when sitting to me he does business with the secretaries and others.' So 'buried in papers' was he that his wife complained she seldom had time for private conversation with him. During the hot months of 1876 and '77, Lytton must have rather dreaded going to his paper-laden desk each morning, for, inevitably awaiting him, would be several long stiff vellum dispatches from District Officers and his staff in the Department of Agriculture and Commerce giving full details of the increasingly alarming famine conditions that existed in the country's central and southern provinces.

If the rains do not fall within this month the *rabi* harvest will fail very greatly. . . . It is of much importance in the Collectorate . . . and there will be scarcity of grass and grain straws. . . . The early crops in many places are being cut for forage. . . . At the weekly market, cattle are offered for sale at nominal prices and find no purchasers. . . . Crime is also on the increase and travellers fear robbery. . . .

By October Lytton learned that crops which should have fully grown were 'scarcely a foot high with not a particle of grain on them,' and that the crop failure was 'throwing on the hands of the authorities many thousands who do not ordinarily work for labour.' A telegram of 24 October 1876 tersely declared: 'If the north-east monsoon should not set in favourably within fifteen days, gravest results. Very heavy Imperial expenditure probably inevitable.'

Lytton kept the Secretary of State, Lord Salisbury, fully informed of the serious situation and requested additional funds for famine relief works such as the repairing and building of water tanks and wells, the improving and constructing of roads and railways that would be equal to carrying supplies from other parts of the country to the stricken provinces.

The winter weather did not much improve the situation, and by the following summer two or three of the southern provinces were 'on the verge of catastrophe', according to a local official's report. Help for the infirm, the aged and children was quite inadequate, the mortality rate was rising fast, and the position was aggravated in some districts by graft and mismanagement. In Madras, 'Money is being flung away broadcast, not going to the right people or places,' Lytton reported. And so, in mid-August of '77, to a salute of thirty-one guns fired from the Peterhoff grounds, Lytton left Simla for the south to inspect the scale of the catastrophe for himself and try to work out a remedy. 'And I must say that in so doing, Lord Lytton does not consult his own convenience,' Prinsep remarked.

The horrors of starvation must have seemed almost unbelievable to those living within the security of the cool and well-watered hills, for whom, Prinsep noted, the only trouble about food was its monotony: 'Everywhere you get the same thing to eat. Preserved salmon or whitebait, the same soup and entrées – and nearly the same company.' So many jars and tins of preserved European delicacies were required for every decent tiffin and supper – it made Prinsep understand the reason for 'the wealth of Messrs Crosse & Blackwell'.

For, however high the cost, the British in India continued to import a great many things from dear Home. Not only the familiar jams and sauces from Crosse & Blackwell, but clothes from the most fashionable Saville Row tailors, chinaware and furnishings from the best West End stores were all sent regularly to even the remotest out-station – for 'native products' were considered vastly inferior in every particular. And this was symptomatic of their general attitude, for the country's political and social affairs received scant serious attention from the average Anglo-Indian and there was little real communication between them and the Indian community. This was so even in places like Calcutta and Bombay where most of the European-educated Indians lived, and it was even more true in the hill-stations where most of the indigenous population were servants or tradespeople. Consequently, wrote satirist Aberigh-Mackay, 'At a bureaucratic Simla dinner-party the abysses of ignorance that yawn below the company on every Indian topic are appalling.'

The ancient culture of the country, the rich intensities of its popular religions also remained a closed book to most Anglo-Indians; its music a meaningless noise in their ears, its erotic art and sculpture a disquieting shock, while the apparent irrationality, passivity, mysteriousness of the Indian outlook on life fretted and secretly rather terrified them. As an anonymous writer in a *Chambers' Magazine* of the 1880s put it:

The English in India are wise to surround themselves as far as they can with an English atmosphere and to defend themselves from the magic of the land by sport, games, clubs and the chatter of fresh-imported girls and by fairly regular attendance at Church. They are probably following instincts of self-preservation.

In Simla, where Anglo-Indians' main preoccupation was the preservation of their physical and mental health, the magic of the land was kept almost totally at bay and native culture was kept firmly in its inferior place. At the opening of the Simla Fine Art Society's Exhibition of 'Native Industrial Art' held at the residence of Ravenswood in 1880, the Society's President condescendingly explained that, of course, all the greatest artists were Europeans, such as Michelangelo and Raphael, nevertheless,

There are a vast number of useful objects which native artisans can not only be brought to manufacture excellently well, but on which the application of the resources of Native indigenous ornament are both agreeable and suitable.

Thus cautioned not to expect too much, the residents of Simla flocked to the Exhibition and perhaps took unexpected, though generally uninformed pleasure in the beautiful objects there displayed: a pair of enamelled mongo birds from Jaipur, curved daggers from Khanjar inlaid with turquoise and ruby, carved sandalwood boxes lent by the Maharaja of Udaipur, horn backscratchers from Veerana, poppy-shaped snuff boxes, delicately foliated metal vessels made in Moradabad, lacquer-painted toys from Surat, 'instruments like paper knives carved with elephant handles and used for relieving pressure of a tight turban', explained the catalogue, and some fine silver-chased work from Lucknow that was unfortunately 'utterly misapplied to European designs for salt and pepper castors.'

That year of the Exhibition was the last of the Lyttons' Viceroyalty.

At home, Disraeli's Government suddenly fell, Gladstone became Prime Minister, and so Lord Ripon was sent out post-haste by the Liberals to replace Lytton and reverse the latter's 'forward policy' in Afghanistan – a country that was still apt to give the ruling heads at Simla sleepless nights. Usually, Viceregal changeovers took place with due planning and ceremony in Calcutta; but on this occasion Lytton, who had not expected such an abrupt change of fortune, was spending his usual summer season at Simla, and the new Viceroy went directly thither to take up his duties. Lytton was renowned for suave courtliness of manner, and 'never for a moment showed his chagrin at being deposed so unexpectedly . . . he treated the incoming Viceroy as a guest,' wrote a Simla guidebook admiringly.

Because Peterhoff was far too small for any kind of formal investiture, Lytton had arranged for a *shamiana* (a square, flat-roofed tent) to be erected on the lawn for the occasion. Into it crowded all the station's VIPs both civilian and military, arrayed in their most splendid outfits to await Ripon's arrival. It was extremely hot and stuffy in that tent, noted one lady who was present, and everyone was very fretful when, at five o'clock, Lord Ripon eventually came hurrying down the strip of red cloth laid on the grass for him. He looked rather dishevelled and travel-stained and was apparently rather embarrassed by the whole situation for he kept trying to explain to Lytton that he really hadn't wanted to come out at all, that he felt he must apologise for the whole business and was only obeying orders. . . . Lord Lytton deflected his apologies skilfully by presenting to him one dignitary after another, including a Sikh Raja whose politely bowing turban poor Lord Ripon nearly knocked off. But at last the ceremony – the most historically noteworthy ever to be performed on a Simla lawn, claimed the guidebook – was over.

For Lady Lytton it was, as she wrote in her diary, 'rather a dreadful day'. Following the tiresome ceremony in the *shamiana*, she dressed for dinner in her bedroom that evening as usual, but then she never saw it again. For, after the meal, 'We had to leave and when it came to starting off from the old house I felt it a good deal and very nearly broke down, with so many cordial shakes of the hand.' By midnight the Lyttons had been quietly spirited away in jampans to stay with Lord Frederick Roberts in his residence called Snowdon, leaving Lord Ripon as the official occupant of Peterhoff.

The general character of Lord Ripon's Viceroyalty was less stylish and jolly than that of the Lyttons. Moreover, Lord Ripon made himself unpopular among the majority of Anglo-Indians by his declared intention of promoting 'the small beginnings of independent political life', and by his support of the controversial Ilbert Bill which proposed giving native magistrates equal authority with European ones in the courts. At Simla, the Ripons were remembered chiefly for their charitable good works, including the founding of Ripon Hospital, and for their conversion of a small room in Peterhoff to a Roman Catholic chapel. It was also held against them that their chaplain, Father Kerr, wrote the oft-quoted description of Simla: 'The whole place is a make-shift. Government House a shooting box. Government offices there are none. You would be surprised to see how the work is carried on.' Ripon must have taken his chaplain's point, for it was during his reign that several new government offices were erected on sites formerly occupied by some of the town's oldest and most charming private houses. The offices, which were of concrete set up on bald iron girders, were generally considered to be too dominating, very ugly and threatened the already overcrowded hillsides near the centre with complete collapse.

The earnest liberalism of Ripon's tenure was somewhat mitigated, in Simla's eyes, by the presence on his staff of Lord William Beresford, popularly known as Bill. Lord William had been one of the brightest sparks among Lord Lytton's effervescent a-d-c's and was early renowned for his charm and wit. He was an excellent and reckless horseman, and his steeds – Oliver Twist, Lucifer, Firetail – cantered to almost inevitable victory over the Annandale turf every season. He was an enthusiastic believer in Simla's future prosperity, and it was he who initiated the widening of the road round Mount Jakko and was reputedly the first to drive a phaeton and pair completely around that much-regarded peak. When the Gaiety Theatre went into a temporary doldrums in the early '80s, Lord William paid off some of its debts, reserving for his personal guests two of its gilded boxes – invitations to his select post-performance champagne suppers were eagerly sought.

Beresford was also good at his job which, as Military Secretary to Lord Ripon, consisted of arranging, with due regard for precedent and protocol, a great number of official receptions, up-country tours, pigsticking excursions, hunting trips, picnics and other Viceregal entertainments, together with the deployment of subordinates, servants, and the transportation of vast quantities of equipment and baggage. For, whatever the personal inclinations of the Viceregal pair, the busyness of their official entertainment schedule constantly increased. This was partly due to the ever-growing numbers of noteworthy visitors from Home who, as means of travelling became easier and faster, included India in their itineraries. Among the usual seasonal arrivals were the young sprigs of various European royal houses, presidents of London-based commercial, scientific and academic institutions, retired military and business men and members of surveying expeditions who, following the new fashion for mountain exploration, would then go hurrying off towards the higher reaches of the Himalayas followed by retinues of bearers.

The most disliked arrival among Anglo-Indians themselves was the peripatetic Member of Parliament come out to report to his constituents on conditions in the unknown East and usually full of theories about the need for political and social reform in India. The typical 'Parliamentary globetrotter' is 'yearly more vigorous, more inquisitive, more corpulent, more disposed to make a note of it,' according to the writer Sara Jeanette Duncan who lived in an Elizabethan-style house called Holcombe near the Mall during the 1880s and wrote a delightful little book about it all called *The Simple Adventures of a Memsahib*. The M.P. was moreover, and especially during periods of Liberal office, very inclined to loudly and publicly deplore the 'frivolous indolence' of Anglo-Indian pursuits in places such as Simla, and to expostulate on 'the wrongs, the sufferings, the grievances under British rule of his two hundred and fifty-five million fellow subjects in India.'

Much more agreeable, in Miss Duncan's opinion, was another recent addition to the globetrotting genus – that of the 'well-connected spinster' who was travelling in independent respectability in a way that was simply not permitted to earlier generations of Victorian ladies. An early representative on the Simla scene was Miss Constance Gordon Cumming who stayed there in 1884. Like others of her kind, Miss Cumming took an intelligent interest in the history and customs of the countries she visited and was prone to purple passages about the beauties of untamed Nature, together with coolly perceptive observations on the conventions of British colonial society.

The modest villas inhabited by those colonials who regularly frequented Simla were, Miss Cumming decided, 'A good deal like Swiss chalets with a strong family likeness to each other.' Perhaps so, but, once weathered and matured, they had considerable charm. Their shaded verandahs were furnished with bamboo chairs and tables, potted geraniums, fuchsias and ferns in hanging baskets; there the ladies sat, sewed and chatted about the current affairs of the station, the health of their children, the delinquencies of their servants, the contents of the latest packet of letters from Home. Inside, the furniture would usually have been made by local carpenters skilled in copying designs from illustrated English magazines, and, for decoration, there were water-colour sketches, photographs of absent relatives, sporting trophies, 'native curios'.

The writer Aberigh-Mackay gives a vivid description of one such villa, where dwelt one of the 'classics' on the Simla scene – the 'grass widow':

It is a cottage with a verandah, built on a steep slope and buried deep in shrubbery and trees. Within all is plain, but exquisitely neat. A wood fire is burning gaily and the kindly tea-tray is at hand. It is five o'clock. Clean servants move silently about with hot water, cake etc. . . . . A little boy, hostage from Pappa in the warm plains below, is sitting pensively after the fashion of Anglo-Indian children in a little chair – his bearer crouches behind him. The widow, in a tea-gown dully splendid with tropical vegetation in neutral tints, holds a piece of chocolate in her hand while she leans back in her *fauteuil* convulsed with laughter. . . .

He says no more about the child, but Constance Cumming was rather scandalised to see as many as eleven servants attending to the needs of one sickly-looking baby. Indeed, those children who stayed in Simla 'to get the roses back in their cheeks', as the phrase went, were apparently over-spoiled even by Anglo-Indian standards. They were dressed, fed and carried about by amahs and bearers as if they were oriental royalty and, as a result, wrote another critical lady visitor, were 'the most dislikeable and rodworthy little mortals imaginable . . . full of conceit and effrontery.' The boys refused to stick at their lessons, and the girls were allowed to go to balls when they were no more than twelve years old and soon took on the 'worst airs and graces of vain womanhood'.

For Miss Cumming, the most enjoyable aspects of Simla life were the unfamiliar ones: the sight of a colourful crowd of jampanees waiting outside Christchurch every Sunday morning, gossiping, smoking and playing 'knuckle-bone'. Each household of any standing had its own particular jampanee-livery; only those attached to the Viceregal establishment were officially allowed to wear the imperial scarlet, but many of the others sported elaborate combinations of 'purple and emerald with light blue trimmings', of 'bright yellow tunics and claret-coloured caps'.

The chief jampanees, known as 'mates', wore magnificent long coats and bright turbans and their duties included trimming the household lamps and carrying calling cards. These were printed name cards which every new arrival in Simla was obliged to take round to the 'not-at-home boxes' that were nailed to trees near the paths leading to each house. The unwritten rule was that such calls should be made between noon and two pm – which involved the newcomer in much hot and fruitless journeying, for the ladies of the house seldom actually received people during these hours and the leaving of the card was merely a polite formality. Such a custom was pleasurable enough in earlier days, when Simla society was small and intimate, but, Edward Buck comments, it later 'developed into a serious social nuisance.' Eventually, ' "box-hunting" instead of visiting became the rule', for no one had time to actually call on all the people that politeness demanded. Still, it gave ladies and jampanees something to do, and when it was suggested that the habit be changed or dropped altogether, 'innumerable complications, heart-burnings and squabbles' resulted, according to Buck.

Another of the chief jampanee's duties was marching ahead with a lantern on night-time rides. And how romantic and beautiful it was, Miss Cumming thought, to be borne home after some late evening party along four miles of dark, silent, winding hill-path. The 'rays of the mate's lantern showing here a shower of fallen crimson rhododendron petals on a patch of maidenhair fern', a tree shrouded in creepers, and, flitting above it, 'night-beetles like glow worms with transparent tails'.

Next morning, at daybreak, the first sound she heard would be the tap on the nearby window – it was the old *gwala* (cowman) bringing a bowl of sweet milk for the children of the house. Then up to an Indian-style 'little breakfast' of tea, toast and fresh fruit on the verandah; swallows skimming round the eaves in the cool blue morning light and, below, the bheesties trundling up the path from the nearby ravine bearing filled water-skins on their backs. Later, perhaps, travelling merchants would arrive and tumble their tempting wares on the verandah steps – shawls and cloaks made from the silky hair of the Kashmiri goats; peacock-feather fans, gold and silver embroidered cushions from the bazaars of Delhi; painted wooden toys, apricot jams and animal-skin rugs from the people of the hills.

All this was exciting and novel enough and Miss Cumming was thrilled too with the beauty of the place for, in her time, one could still strike off on the narrow woodland paths and be alone with 'the magical silence of mountain and tree'. But, as several visitors before and after her, Miss Cumming was slightly disappointed by the very sophistication of the Simla social scene. It was all

Too silky and perfumed to be in keeping with the wild mountain scenery. Fancy coming to these uttermost ends of the earth to be pursued by Paris fashions; satins, velvets, the 'newest thing' in bonnets which have just been sent to the wearer by pattern post – to say nothing of the last thing in white satin boots! . . .

But while, on the one hand, Simla seemed rather too tamed and urbanised for the passing globetrotter in search of the more mysterious East, its comparative lack of civilised amenities quite surprised those members of the international diplomatic corps who found they were expected to live there for half the year. Among them, in 1884, were Lord and Lady Dufferin, who were later characterised as 'an eminently well-behaved couple and fond of rational amusement.' Their previous postings had included Montreal and St Petersburg and, used to such large-scale grandeurs, Lady Harriot Georgina, Marchioness of Dufferin and Ava, or 'Lady D—', as she was often called, immediately decided that Simla was a small-town, claustrophobic sort of place. As for Peterhoff, though 'very suitable for any family desiring to lead a family and not an

Lady Dufferin, Vicereine 1884-8.

official life' it was 'very unfit for a vice-regal establishment'. At the back of the house was about 'a yard to spare before you tumble down a precipice, and in front there is just room for a tennis-court before you go over another.'

She was also highly critical of the state of the roads for, 'Walking, riding, driving all seem to be indulged in at the risk of one's life'. This was rather hard, for, during the two previous Viceroyalties, the whole of the Mall, extending some ten miles round Mount Jakko, had been sufficiently smoothed and widened to carry wheeled traffic. In consequence, the jinrickshaw that had been invented in Japan about 1870 and rapidly gained popularity throughout the East began to appear on the Simla scene. Compared to the 'back-aching abomination' of the jampan, the jinrickshaw, which Lady Dufferin describes as a 'sort of bath-chair pushed and pulled by four men', was quite comfortable. It usually had padded seats, an oilskin hood and arm-rests – but it did tilt at most alarming angles when negotiating the steep hill-paths. Anyway, Lady D— found it all quite disconcertingly cramped and precarious at first, and expressed special concern for the poor a-d-c's on her staff who 'are all slipping off the hills in various little bungalows and go through the most perilous adventures to come to dinner'.

In charge of the a-d-c's and their precarious establishments was Lord William Beresford who had again been re-appointed to his position by the new Viceroy. And, said Lady D— approvingly, 'From the highest military affairs in the land, to the mosquito inside His Excellency's curtain or a bolt on my door, all is the business of this invaluable person'. Beresford, a stayer, had become a familiar and generally well-liked character on the hill-station scene. He had acquired a poodle called Ponto with an eye for the ladies which, according to rumour, was as roving as his master's – who remained, nevertheless, an eligible and flirtatious bachelor; but apparently a respectable one, for 'The nice little church at Simla used to echo with the sound of Lord William's clinking spurs' as he walked up the aisle with the collection plate every Sunday morning, according to his admiring biographer.

When there were two or more guests at Peterhoff, which was quite often, the extras were put up at 'Inverarm', Beresford's comfortable house nearby, where there was, naturally, a first-class stable, lawn tennis courts for the younger set and sideboards gleaming 'with his many trophies of the chase and sport generally'. Still, it was quite ridiculous that the country's leading family could offer overnight hospitality to so few people and, very soon after his arrival in Simla, Lord Dufferin began to press for the building of a more spacious and impressive Viceregal residence.

'D— and I visited Observatory Hill which is the site Lord Lytton chose for the new Government House,' recorded Lady D—in the spring of 1885. 'At Calcutta it was proposed that we should alter this cottage into a fitting Vice-regal residence, but the moment we saw the proximity of our precipice and the smallness of the house, we began to think that it would be a mistake to build here and now that we have seen the new site we are convinced of it'. The site was named after an 'Observatory House' which was built there in 1844 by one Colonel J. Boileau who set up an observatory 'well fitted with magnetic instruments'. There were two Boileau brothers in the station at this time, both apparently of such eccentric and remarkable habits that the western end of Simla was named Boileau-gunge in their memory for decades afterwards.

At any rate, 'There is a splendid view from the hill and a large space of vacant ground to build on,' Lady D— decided – and every reason for beginning as soon as possible if the Dufferins were to enjoy the finished creation. Lord Dufferin himself supervised and constantly amended the overall plans for the new building, which proved rather a trial for the Public Works Department, but it was, wrote Edward Buck, 'his one chief distraction from the heavy and serious business with which his Viceroyalty was occupied'.

Certainly Lord Dufferin, a somewhat aloof man with a proven reputation as a skilled diplomatist, had much to occupy his mind, most especially the growing signs of political and social awareness among younger, educated Indians. The first Indian National Congress was held during the first year of his Viceroyalty, and one of its prime English movers was Allan Octavian Hume, a former Customs Commissioner who, on retiring to Simla, devoted himself to the promotion of liberal ideals for Indian self-government. Dufferin himself expressed some tentative sympathy with the new trend, but he also sometimes made reference to the mysterious decrees of Providence which had ordered Britain to take on the government of India.

While her husband wrestled with his new responsibilities, Lady Dufferin found herself settling down quite happily after all to Simla's patterns. 'I really think it is a very nice place and that it is growing larger in my estimation,' she wrote after being there a month. And, to negotiate the narrow unmade paths that were not suitable for carriage or jinrickshaw, she acquired a mule called Begum. It was a sensible, useful creature with a reassuring look in her eye on even the steepest incline, and, 'When she wears a blue necklace and has a few red tassels about her she will look lovely'.

The invaluable Beresford was full of good ideas on passing the time pleasantly – one of them being the annual excursion he always organised to the Sipi Fair, held in a neighbouring valley. The path to it 'was such a zigzag one,' Lady D— noted, 'that I felt as if I was trying to dance a quadrille on horseback, there were such sharp turns in it, bringing one face to face with one's partner either above or below'. But the Fair itself was well worth it:

About twenty merry-go-rounds all revolving at once, carrying basketfulls of men, women and children round and round through the air; there were little shops selling the latest things in the way of novelties from Birmingham [sic]; there were serpent charmers and performing monkeys and men beating tom-toms; there was an elephant beautifully got up and a little brass god seated in an arm-chair receiving small coin.

The Simla-based Europeans mingled with the crowds of 'picturesque hill-folk' all in their best bright jackets, cloth caps, satin trousers and 'the heads, noses, ears, throats, arms and ankles of the young women were laden with jewellery.' Luncheon for the Viceregal party had been laid on by the a-d-c's and quite a banquet it was, 'with tables and chairs and silver and every luxury that we are accustomed to at home.' It was a real 'poggle-khana' in fact – that is, a 'fools' meal', as the Indians described the incorrigible and incomprehensible British habit of eating out of doors by choice.

Other seasonal events capably managed by Lord William were the various race-meetings, which took place on a much enlarged Annandale course. Captains starved themselves to jockey-weight in order to compete for the Viceroy's Cup or the Mooltan Stakes, and there were Ladies' Hack Races, steeplechases and jinrickshaw races, with young ladies in rickshaws urging their four native pullers towards the winning post. To add to the fun Lord William had invented the Victoria Cross Race. Its competitors had first to race to pick up a dummy figure dressed as a nurse, soldier, ayah, war correspondent etc. from the 'field of battle', and then canter back to the winning post holding the figure on their saddle.

For the pleasure of race-days was just that – no one took them too seriously. There was no grandstand and people simply sat about on the hillsides under the trees to watch the events and, wrote Lady D—:

Seeing all one's intimate friends got up as jockeys and all the riding horses of the place appearing as racers, is amusing; and then the course is small and the performers are never out of sight and they look like toys galloping round a board, and one is able to get up a special interest either in a well-known man or a particular horse and so is infected a little by the surrounding excitement.

So it was all very jolly, but Annandale was no longer the romantic, sequestered glen of former years. It was splendid with laid-out formal gardens, and a flat playground for polo and cricket matches, gymkhanas, and 'tilting the ring'. Lady Dufferin's two daughters enjoyed the last game tremendously, and they and the 'Two Misses Stewarts . . . all gal-

loped about, lances in hand, their hats falling off and their hair all dishevelled, looking very energetic and very much amused'. The young men, meanwhile, took to tent-pegging, riding wildly with two ponies or jumping hurdles.

After the day-time Annandale romps, a visit to the Gaiety Theatre was often the order of the evening. In 1887 a new Gaiety was opened in the same building as the Town Hall: 'It is a very pretty little place,' Lady D— thought, 'and is nicely decorated with pink muslin curtains in each box and gold and white paint. We sit near the stage and not only see the play very well, but all the people in the theatre too, which adds to the amusement.' The first play put on in the new theatre was a comedy called *Time Will Tell*, and the prologue recited at its opening inspired some witty verses that appeared in the *Civil and Military Gazette* and were reputedly written by a young reporter called Rudyard Kipling. In them, Kipling reminded his readers of the Simla theatre's long history for:

> Time, the grim destroyer,
> Already blurs the photos in your foyer . . .

And he goes on to commend the excellence and moral rectitude of its many actors:

> Praise most yourselves – the Perfect and the Chaste.
> Why 'chaste' amusement? Do our morals fail
> Amid the deodars of Annandale?
> Into what vicious vortex do they plunge
> Who dine on Jakko or in Boileaugunge?
> Of course it's 'chaste.' Despite the artless paint,
> And Pimm's best wig, who dares to say it ain't?
> Great Grundy! Does a sober matron sink
> To infamy through rouge and Indian ink?
> Avaunt the thought. As tribute to your taste,
> WE CERTIFY THE SIMLA STAGE IS CHASTE.

Later that season Kipling wrote a prologue himself – for *Lucia di Lammermoor* which was performed on a small stage at the residence of Snowdon and was in aid of Lady Roberts' 'Homes in the Hills' Fund. Kipling's sister, dressed as a nurse, spoke the lines and was generally applauded, for the Kipling family shone with more than average brightness on the Simla social scene at this time.

Kipling usually stayed at Northbank, the property that belonged to Sir Edward Buck, whose nephew wrote Simla's first definitive history. Kipling was fond of the place, which was famed for the troops of monkeys that used to gambol about on the tennis courts in the early mornings. Years later, he apparently wrote to Buck to enquire, 'And do the

Kipling as a young man; a photograph by the Bourne and Shepherd studio.

monkeys still come to the upper bedrooms at Northbank and take the hairbrushes off the table?'

But when his collection of stories *Plain Tales from the Hills* first appeared, it caused considerable offence in some Simla circles. As Edward Buck, a fervently loyal inhabitant of the place, explained

Wonderfully clever as these short stories were, they have, I fear, led many to regard Simla as a town populated by Mrs Hauksbees, by frivolous grass-widows, idle hill captains and the genus known as 'bow-wows', and no writer has perhaps done more than the brilliant genius I have mentioned to give the outside world the idea of Simla as a centre of frivolity, jealousy and intrigue.

This as may be, but certainly Lady Dufferin's detailed journals of her seasons in Simla that appear in her book, *Our Viceregal Life in India*, do suggest that pleasure-seeking was the chief occupation of many of its residents. For only the vagaries of the weather, it seemed, could pour cold water on plans for the next woodland picnic/chocolate and strawberry tea/garden fête/band concert/clay-pigeon shooting/dog show/ Monday Pop/fern-gathering expedition.

The year 1887 was particularly festive because it was Queen Victoria's Jubilee at Home. Lady Roberts held a Jubilee Ball at Snowdon, and the ballroom was decorated with blue and gold shields bearing the names of Sir Frederick's fields of battle and, on the stage, 'a trophy made of bayonets, a great "50" in the centre of it and the word "Jubilee" below.' Not to be outdone, the Fancy Dress Ball that the Dufferins held at Peterhoff was acclaimed as one of the most brilliant ever. The irrepressible Lord William was much in evidence 'as the most perfect Chelsea Pensioner, hobbling in on a stick and coughing painfully'. Then there was Mr Rosen as a 'magnificent Afghan' with black-dyed beard and 'the peculiar Afghanish walk that he puts on'; Mrs Gordon, the a-d-c's sister-in-law, looked quite scintillating as a gold and white Gadfly with wings on her shoulders and head; Mr Elliott, the Commissioner of Assam, wore the real outfit of a Manipur chieftain; Miss Gough was 'an adorable White Cat with swansdown trimmings and little pussy's ears'; and Lord Dufferin amazed them all by making a brief appearance so convincingly disguised as an Arab gentleman that his wife didn't recognise him when he spoke to her.

With so much innocent enjoyment going on, it seemed rather mean of a visiting Archdeacon to preach a trenchant sermon in the church one Sunday on 'our lives of dissipation here'. This caused considerable heart-searching, and Lady D— had to admit, 'It is quite true that the atmosphere of the place is one of pleasure-seeking'. However, as she hastens to explain, her own time was not totally idled away. She started a Work Society among the women whereby each undertook to produce six articles of clothing a year to be donated to two orphanages, the hospital and a nearby leper asylum; she took regular lessons in Hindustani; she played the organ and helped to train the local choir; and, more than all this, she spent much of her energy at Simla in the creation and organisation of The Countess of Dufferin's Fund for Supplying Female Medical Aid to the Women of India.

The religious laws of the country did not permit women in purdah to be treated by male doctors, and, as no women doctors existed, many such women received no qualified medical help in times of illness or childbirth. Lady D's fund was set up therefore to train numbers of Indian women as doctors, midwives and nurses who could alleviate the situation. It was another typical manifestation of the social concern and growing enthusiasm for good works that was prevalent in later Victorian times. To one of Emily Eden's stamp such a concept as the Dufferin Fund would have been inconceivable.

Equally inconceivable to Miss Eden would have been a Viceregal Residence in 'dear little Simla' of the scale and magnificence that was built on Observatory Hill during the Dufferins' period of office. On 15 July 1887 Lady D— recorded that she and her husband went to watch the building going on and

The workpeople are very amusing to look at, especially the young ladies in necklaces, bracelets, earrings, tight cotton trousers, turbans with long veils hanging down their backs – and a large earthenware basin of mortar on their heads. They walk about with the carriage of empresses, and seem as much at ease on the top of the roof as on the ground floor; most picturesque masons they are.

Before the Dufferins left Simla that season they provided a feast for the thousand or so workers engaged in the house construction, and the workers provided them with some 'native entertainments' in return.

There were men with red masks, golden helmets, glittering jackets, swords and bare brown legs, jumping about aimlessly in the manner of clowns. There were long-bearded and crowned pantaloons; there were imitation nautch-girls; there were men dressed as Langours, the costume consisting of cotton-wool glued to the naked skin. . . .

There were wrestling and fencing matches, the singing of 'laudatory songs to the Viceroy', and the *pièce de résistance* was the arrival of a 'large wooden tiger borne aloft on men's shoulders' with a 'Goddess of Devi' behind it. By the next year, the Dufferins promised themselves, the structure would be completed and they would be able to look out of their grand new oriel windows, from which 'Simla scenery is seen to greater advantage than from any other place I know.'

It did not turn out quite so smoothly however, for when the Dufferins first got back to the station the following May, the edifice was still 'in a very unpromising condition'. Stone cutters were busily working on the walling, which was of limestone quarried about five miles away and brought to the site on mule–back, and the electric generators, which were eventually to illuminate the establishment's thousand or so lights, were only just being dragged up the hill. But, spurred by the Dufferins' return, the colourful and obliging workpeople redoubled their efforts and by mid-July the house was beginning to 'look very well'.

The entrance hall was its great feature: a broad teak staircase with walnut balusters leading from it to a lofty gallery, and both hall and gallery being open to the top of the three-storey-high house giving 'an appearance of space and height which is very grand'. Much of the house was furnished by Messrs Maple & Co of London, who sent out assistants especially for the purpose, and Lady D— particularly loved the effect they had created in the big drawing-room, 'furnished with gold and brown silks and with large bow windows and a small round tower recess off it.'

From the recess, one could look down on the light yellows and greys of the ballroom, and a gallery from the ballroom led into the imposing dining-room, which had sumptuous crimson curtains and 'high panelling of teak, along the top of which are shields with the arms and coronets of all the Viceroys and of some celebrated Governor-Generals, and above that, Spanish leather in rich dark colours.' For the Viceroy, there was a 'rather dark and serious looking' study; for the Vicereine, a boudoir with a 'tower-room recess which is nearly all glass'. In short, it was all very spacious and splendid, and perfectly in tune with the times, for, as Buck points out,

Society in Simla had grown so much that whereas in Lord Lytton's day at Peterhoff, the official parties did not exceed four hundred persons, over eight hundred are now invited to the State Ball at Viceregal Lodge.

To cope with so much large-scale official entertaining, the below-stairs kitchen wing of the Lodge was, sensibly, five storeys high and unusually well appointed by the standards of Anglo-Indians – for many of their household kitchens consisted of no more than a blackened charcoal range, a few cupboards and dubious cooking pots tucked away in a smoky hut some distance from the dining-room.

But on Observatory Hill there was none of that. There were separate rooms for storing Table Linen, Plate, China and Glass, and the Chief Steward had his own bedroom and sitting-room near at hand. On the Kitchen Floor there was a Pastry Pantry, a Cook's Room, a Smoke Jack for Roasting near the white-tiled kitchen, which contained a range

$44' \times 20'$. Below this again was a well-equipped laundry and, wrote Lady D—

How the *dhobies* will like it at first I don't know. What they are accustomed to is to squat on the brink of a cold stream and there to flog and batter our wretched garments against the hard stones until they think them clean. Now they will be condemned to warm water and soap and mangles and ironing and drying rooms, and they will probably think it all very unnecessary and will perhaps faint with the heat.

Yet lower below stairs was a sweepers' room, 'two lounges for the under-servants' near the furnaces, an enormous wine cellar, an Empty Cases Room, a Lumber Room and a Bottling Passage.

By 23 July 1888 everything was more or less *in situ*, even though the grounds were still mere heaps of builders' rubble, and the Dufferins moved in. Lady D— went up first and busied herself with the arranging of furniture and draperies. Her husband and daughters joined her at dinner-time

when everything was brilliantly lighted up by the electric light. It certainly is very good and the lighting up and putting out of the lamps is so simple that it is quite a pleasure to go round one's room touching a button here and there, and to experiment with various amounts of light.

After dinner, feeling a little strange and selfconscious, they all sat in the smaller drawing-room, 'which is still a little stiff and company-like, but it will soon get into our ways and be more comfortable.'

A fortnight later the Dufferins held their first formal entertainment in the new Lodge, for 'all the Council and "personages" of Simla':

First we had a large dinner – sixty-six people at one long table. The electric light is enough, but as candelabras ornament the table we had some on it. At one end of the room there is a sideboard covered with gold plate etc. and at the other end, double doors were open and across the ballroom one saw the band which played during the dinner.

Few people were as uncritically admiring of the new Viceregal Lodge as its first residents, the Dufferins – who only spent part of one summer there before their period of office ended. In less elevated circles the story was put about that Indian income tax was introduced in 1886 to help pay for it, and others who stayed there likened it to a Scottish Hydro, Pentonville Prison and, because of its oriel windows and crenellated tower, an oversize and pretentious medieval castle.

But pretentiousness, a certain heavy-footed, opulent flamboyance was characteristic of the High Raj, which reached its peak during the decade following the Dufferins' departure. The trouble was that, in Simla, as so often elsewhere, its thriving prosperity and its importance as the summer headquarters of an increasingly powerful government had the effect of destroying so much that had been charming, quaint, small-scale and intimate.

Long gone were the days of Lord Lytton when, according to Aberigh-Mackay, the Supreme Council used to foregather 'on Sunday evenings after tea and catechism for riddles and forfeits in the snug little cloak-room parlour at Peterhoff'. In those times the Public Works Department was quartered in Herbert House, the Foreign Office in Valentines, the Adjutant-General in Strawberry Hill and the Military in Dalzell House – from which, in yet earlier days, Captain G. D. Thomas, who made his admirable sketches of the district in the 1840s, looked out upon 'purple and shadowy dells', 'dark, dense woods' and 'dewy English wild flowers'.

Half a century later the Government of India Press had its mighty being on the site formerly occupied by Tally-Ho Hall, where a sporting Major Goad, who once owned thirty-three Simla properties, used to entertain on truly lavish old English fashion, and exercise his pack of hounds each morning in the valley of Annandale. 'As the visitor to Simla proceeds down the Mall towards Viceregal Lodge he is confronted by a great masonry pile, mainly constructed from stone quarried from the Sanjouli bazaar which constitutes the new Civil Secretariat Building', Buck explains. On its small eminence formerly stood the prominent land-mark of Gorton Castle, quite near the original Kennedy House. It used to belong to one Colonel T. Colyear who was also owner of a large number of properties and who scandalised local opinion in the '60s by having twice married native ladies.

Another of Simla's best-loved residences was Benmore, and its history, as chronicled by Buck, epitomises the changing fate of many similar estates. It was built near Barnes Court by a military officer in the days when Lord William Hay was Superintendent of the Hill States. In 1869 it was bought by Herr Felix von Goldstein, a professional musician and Bandmaster to the Viceroy. He added a ballroom and skating rink to the house, for 'rinking' was a popular amusement at the time and one of the few forms of exercise that was permitted to young ladies as well as men. Goldstein's spirited renderings of the familiar waltzes and polkas of the '70s and '80s made Benmore 'the Kursaal of Simla'; Rudyard Kipling wrote in romantic mood:

> Eyes of blue – the Simla hills
> Silvered with the moonlight hoar;
> Pleading of the waltz that thrills,
> Dies and echoes round Benmore.

But, when the new Town Hall was built which offered to the general public 'a collection of places of amusement' including a fine new ball-room, Goldstein prudently sold his property to the Punjab Government.

Subsequently it was occupied either in turn or concurrently, by the offices of the Inspectors-General of Police, Prisons and Civil Hospitals; by the Director of Public Instruction, the Sanitary Commissioner, the Judge Advocate, the Director of Education, the Consulting Architect of the Government of India, the Chief Inspector of Explosives and the Director of Archeology. Later still, when the even more modern government offices were completed, the parts of old Benmore that had withstood the officials' occupation were demolished altogether. As for the new buildings, the best you could say about them, and Mr Buck tried, was that they were permanent-looking, fireproof and their roofs did not leak.

With so many officials on the spot for most of the year, Simla's every feature became a matter of public record. The geology of Mount Jakko was carefully investigated by a Mr R. D. Oldham of the Survey Department who reached the conclusion that 'the spot now occupied by Simla was a sea on whose surface icebergs floated, melted and dropped the stones which they carried on their surface'; painstaking maps were made showing the location of every large residence, the contours of every twisting hill-path.

The Inspector-General of Forests, pursuing his proper bent, divided the arboreal vegetation between Simla and the snows 'into three strata, of which the main trees in the lowest stratum were the deodar and the white oak; in the middle, the spruce, fir and green oak; at the highest levels, the silver fir and the brown oak.' The Inspector-General also lamented that so much valuable timber had been cut down for house-building and in order to clear ground for the growing of potatoes – which had first been introduced into the area by that amiable Captain Kennedy way back in the 1820s. However, in efforts to supply the growing demands of the station, potato cultivation had got out of hand in the last decade. 'The soil,' reported the Inspector, 'protected no longer by vegetation is now in great part washed away, gaping ravines are forming on every side and soon neither potatoes nor forest will be able to grow.'

For there was no denying that Simla was becoming less lovely than it once had been. The plentiful and varied wild-life had either retreated completely into the further hinterlands or been decimated by too many collectors of private menageries, too many sporting a-d-c's and military men fond of taking pot-shots at whatever moved. Golden eagles were now rarities worthy of special record; pet dogs need no longer fear the leopard; only the ubiquitous monkeys seemed to still proliferate and were 'terribly destructive pests in station gardens', Buck says. Nor did the neighbouring hill-slopes any longer blossom with variegated wild flowers as soon as the summer rains came, for too many roots had been dug up by ladies hoping to improve their herbaceous borders, too many blooms heedlessly picked by servants for the vases of their mistresses' dining tables.

As the town itself became less beautiful, more crowded, those people who could afford it moved further away into the hills – particularly to Mashobra and Mahasu, where only a few extensive estates had been bought in earlier times by rich eccentrics or officials who found the pace of the station too hectic. Commissioners, judges, bank managers, successful hoteliers and military officers now also built residences around the former native settlements, and gave them the same old homely names – Kenilworth, Cosy Nook, Sherwood and Fairlawn.

Many owners of such properties were retired, and so, perforce, spent much of their time in the Simla Club – which was also greatly extended and modernised and could accommodate up to seventy members. Of the typical retired hill-station colonel, Aberigh-Mackay amusingly wrote that,

He rises early, puts on some non-descript white uniform and forage cap and sallies forth to the Club. . . . Now the serious business of life begins – to get through the day. There are six newspapers to read, twelve pegs to drink, four and twenty Madras cheroots to smoke; there is kindly tiffin to linger over, forty winks to take afterwards, a game of billiards, the band on the Mall, dinner, and over all, incessant chatter – old scandals, old jokes and old stories.

With so much nostalgia a-wash among those who had spent many years living in Simla and watching so many changes for the worse, what was the attraction of the place in the 1890s – when it was a more frequented resort than it had ever been? Well, if you were young, socially acceptable and had no memories of earlier days, it offered as much pleasurable fun and interest as ever. To, for example, Miss Caroline Bremner who was there with her sister in the early years of the decade. She stayed at the recently-opened Hotel Cecil, which was centrally located on the site once occupied by a sweet little bungalow called Tendrils Cottage, though Miss Bremner probably did not know it.

No sooner had she unpacked, than she was visited by 'an Indian gentleman . . . or so he appeared' who came to enquire if she would like to rent a villa in the suburbs for the season, or a jinrickshaw with four pullers for a week, or take an excursion along the Great Hindustan Road or to Annandale (with picnic luncheon provided) or just a ride up to the top of Mount Jakko to see the fakir and his monkeys? But, Miss Bremner wrote, 'We had been warned about the natives who live in Simla just to charge high prices to innocent tourists', and she refused all his offers.

She and her sister found it more fun to go out and explore by themselves. They went bowling along in a jinrickshaw that was all fitted up with luxurious cushions, rubber tyres, little glass windows, and they poked about in the main bazaar where most of the shops now had proper counters and glazed fronts instead of the higgledy-piggledy stalls of yesteryear where you couldn't even buy a decent sewing needle.

About five o'clock the thing to take was a stroll along the Mall which was 'thronged with fashionably-dressed ladies and gentlemen all "eating the air", as the Indians say'. Their most popular rendezvous was Peliti's Grand Hotel, which was built on the site of Bentinck Castle and had been opened by that same Italian confectioner who first arrived at the station with Lord Lytton. Lytton's French cook, M. Bansard, had also gone briefly into the hotel business, but had later left the field to the confectioner – who was now a Chevalier and lived in a striking Italian-style house called Villa Carignano. On his hotel's terrace first-rate Italian-style ices and cakes were served and people met to flirt and gossip. 'Everyone seemed to be talking about the last ball or the next one, and which gentleman had danced with which lady, and whether or not it had been proper', Miss Bremner remarked.

It was ever so. An anonymous writer in the *Pioneer* magazine of that year commented:

Nowhere possibly in the world are the passions of human nature laid so open for idssection as they are in the remote hill-stations. . . . The groove into which Anglo-India is forced by circumstances in the plains becomes narrower still in the hills. There, where every advantage of climate is combined with every imaginable beauty of nature, with few housekeeping cares, with many luxuries, with a constant flow of amusements which few save in the richest society at home can attempt to enjoy incessantly – there discontent breeds and jealousy and scandal dominate.

Despite such seething undercurrents, most people always seemed to have a pretty good time – and Miss Caroline Bremner in her time seemed as thoroughly happy in Simla as young Mrs Jane Maria Strachey had once been. She went to a Charity Fête in Annandale held in aid of 'Poor Eurasian Orphans' and won a trinket from a lucky dip in a fish pond; she watched the young gentlemen of the Viceregal staff playing polo, she attended a Ball in the Municipal Buildings where 'a most delicious collation was served in the adjoining supper-room for all who had bought tickets', and she went to see *Floradora* at the Gaiety.

The theatre continued to flourish – counting among its recently successful productions, *The Gondoliers*, *The Gaiety Girl*, *Lady Huntworth's Experiment*, and *A Marriage of Convenience*. The night Miss Bremner was there she was thrilled to see the Viceroy arrive in the gilt royal box accompanied by the Vicereine who 'wore a most becoming gown, for I heard she was attending a reception afterwards. I heard too that they are a very well liked couple and do what they can to promote the good of the station.'

The couple in question, Lord and Lady Lansdowne, were indeed popular. It was Lansdowne who first truly benefited from the use of Viceregal Lodge and he engaged an English gardener, Alfred Parsons, to lay out the grounds with appropriate trees, ornamental shrubs, flower beds, terraces and tennis courts. Quarters for the Clerk of Works, the Chief Electrician, the Household Band, the Personal Bodyguard were dotted unobtrusively about the estate's fringes and a gun housed in a shed near the entrance gates went off at noon each day and fired salutes for specially momentous arrivals and departures. Lady Lansdowne, with the capable Lord William Beresford still as Military Secretary, arranged a number of garden fêtes, afternoon teas, tennis tournaments in the new Viceregal domain every season and, according to the local guidebook, 'her charm of manner as hostess endeared her to all who were fortunate enough to attend them.'

Lord Elgin, who followed Lansdowne into office, could not have been particularly enamoured of Simla for it was he who purchased The Retreat in the village of Mashobra as an escape from the 'despotism of despatch boxes'. When he died suddenly, Lord Nathaniel Curzon was appointed Viceroy and the Curzons first reached Simla in 1899, having travelled up with an enormous retinue of gentlemen on horseback and ladies in rickshaws.

Lady Curzon took an instant dislike to the appearance of the place. 'The Public Works and other buildings have made Simla monstrous,' she wrote. 'All the public buildings are crosses between chalets and readymade iron houses and their fluted roofs cover the hillsides.' As for Viceregal Lodge, well, 'a Minneapolis millionaire would revel in it,' she quipped. She also lamented Messrs Maple's lincrusta and paper ornamentation of the interior. 'It looks at you with pomegranate and pineapple eyes from every wall,' she wrote to her family – and she soon had it replaced with damask, sky-blue and pale green and gold hangings. The most pleasant part of the house, in Curzon's view, was its grounds, and he added to them an avenue of limes and a rose pergola which was such a typical feature of many large Victorian gardens and parks. Lady Curzon felt that, 'A look out of the windows makes up for it all, and I can live on views for five years.'

But the Curzons, who did indeed stay in India for five years, never became converted to the charms of Simla. It was too bustling, 'too public', certainly 'no longer the holiday resort of an Epicurean Viceroy and a pampered government', Curzon decided. He found its pomp and

Lord Curzon, Viceroy of India 1899-1905.

Lady Curzon, Vicereine, née Mary Victoria Leiter of Chicago.

circumstance very small-time and irksome, and he did not admire the calibre of its resident officials, saying that 'hunt the slipper' seemed to be one of their favourite pursuits. The frivolity and gossip of the local society was much too provincial and cosy for his imperial inclinations: 'It is the monotony of the day that kills,' he wrote. 'It is like dining every day in the housekeeper's room with the butler and the lady's maid.'

So the Curzons escaped whenever they could: first to The Retreat at Mashobra, seven miles distant, but, when this proved not retreating enough, Lord Curzon took himself six miles further on to the beautiful mountain spur of Naldera. Here he set up an elaborate camp where he could work and eat outside his tent and where, according to awed and amused observers, he penned some of his most formidable minutes. Servants with large official files strapped on their backs used to ride into the camp, and signallers were stationed there to relay messages to and from Simla by heliograph and (at night) by flashing lamps. In this way, Curzon used to boast that, if there was a mild difference of opinion concerning Indian policy in the House of Lords, he would know of it in his Himalayan fastness within a matter of hours.

In November of 1903, communications between Simla and the outside world were eased and hastened by the introduction of the most up-to-date and long-wished-for of Simla's modern amenities: a railway from Kalka which climbed up the precipitous heights where only tongas and bullock carts had gone before. The engineering skill that went into its construction was a matter of considerable local pride. Wrote Buck:

Through its length of sixty miles it runs in a continuous succession of reverse curves of 120 feet radius, in and out along valleys and spurs, flanking mountains, rising to six and seven thousand feet above sea level, the steep gradients being three feet in a hundred. The works of construction involved are of the first magnitude, comprising 107 tunnels, aggregating five miles in length, numerous lofty arched viaducts, aggregating one and three-quarter miles and innumerable cuts and stone walls.

As one approached the vicinity of Simla itself, the familiar landmarks – which most of the passengers had read about, if not already seen – were visible from the train windows: Mount Jakko with its widened, completed circular road and its tiers of small villas still threatening to tumble off the slopes; Viceregal Lodge high on Observatory Hill, a flag fluttering from its medieval-looking tower when the Viceroy was in residence; Christchurch which, as the guidebook informed them, now had six new bells and a Tudor-style porch and a chancel window with a fresco surrounding it designed by Mr Lockwood Kipling; those ponderous, concrete slabs of the government and municipal offices – with a Superintendent of Railways now added to the ever-extending list of functioning departments.

Christchurch, Simla: the Tudor porch.

From the time of the railway's opening, the world of Simla became ever more open, more public, more casual. Its hotels were more numerous and larger – the Hotel Metropole and the Kensington, in addition to the Grand and the Cecil; on the outskirts, Ivanhoe and Windermere Houses among others, and Elysium Hotel, presumably a delicate compliment to the shades of the Misses Eden. By the end of the year that the railway came, there were some 1,400 European-style dwellings in Simla and new ones were still being built; the irregular crescent of the town extended fully six miles in length, each of its various suburbs called by distinguishing names such as Barra (Great) Simla, Chota (Little) Simla, Prospect Hill, Boileaugunge, Jakko. Its summer population 'averaged 38,000 souls, of whom about 7,000 are Europeans and Eurasians' noted Edward Buck, in whom one distinctly senses some nostalgia for the small-town days of private parties and concerts in cosy drawing-rooms, and too-full houses where everyone knew everyone else. Now, it was no longer practicable for newcomers to even pay their formal respects to all other residents on arrival. For, when fresh loads of visitors might arrive by every train, nobody quite knew anymore who everyone else was. . . .

The Indian hill-station, writes Mr A. King, in Volume 26 No. 3 of the journal *Social Action*, was a continuation in an alien setting of the English-spa concept and a place 'where the elite and aspirants met and participated in established social rituals'; their main characteristic was 'the temporary patronage of their occupants'; their central parades or malls were 'designed to encourage inter-action and the accommodation of personal display'. Hill-stations served and reinforced the 'values and customs of a colonial community' and catered for its religious and recuperative needs; they provided both a picturesque backdrop for recreation and a strategic base for surveillance of possibly troublesome native territory. As such they were 'a form of socio-spatial organisation peculiar to colonial urban development.'

It all makes them sound rather sinister and deeply exploitative. Perhaps they were. Undeniably they were all, like Simla, the repository for a rich collection of memories that haunted generations of Anglo-Indian memories years after they had left the country: the whizz of the arrow to the target in the shady glen and the click of the croquet mallet on the lawn; the rays of the jampanees' lantern jogging along a dark hill-path; the strains of the waltz through the open windows of Benmore's ballroom, and the waking-up thrill of the Snowy Range on a clear golden morning; the comfort of basket chairs on quiet verandahs and the clop of horses' hooves along the Mall; the sound of the first Spring cuckoo one has heard for several years; the aching-sweet homesickness of seeing the Viceregal pergola of roses in the rain.

Photography in nineteenth-century India
Ray Desmond

Only a few years after its invention in Europe photography was taken up in India by enthusiastic amateurs like the army surgeon, John McCosh, who used his camera during the 2nd Sikh War in 1848–49. Its popularity led to the formation of the Photographic Society of Bombay in 1854, followed by similar societies in Calcutta and Madras two years later. Commercial photographers established themselves in the larger cities, and also in hill-stations such as Simla where T. Reinecke and C. W. De Rusett were probably the first. Reinecke, a founder member of the Bengal Photographic Society with a studio in Calcutta, visited Simla every season from about the mid 1850s. About the same time De Rusett threw up his job as an assistant with the firm of Jeffrey and Company, tailors and habit-makers in Simla, and set himself up as a photographer. Some years later however he was working as a builder, presumably because he could no longer earn a living solely from photography after the arrival of other competitors such as J. Craddock and Shepherd and Robertson. Shepherd and Robertson, who founded a photographic firm in Agra about 1862, moved to Simla about 1864. Shortly afterwards Samuel Bourne joined them as a partner.

Bourne is one of the great names in Indian photography. Formerly a bank clerk in Nottingham and a keen photographer, he came to Calcutta from England early in 1863 and almost immediately headed for Simla. His first glimpse of the hill-station disappointed him.

A mass of apparently tumbledown native dwellings on the top of a ridge, with bungalows scattered here and there on the sides of a mountain covered partially with fir trees, without a single yard of level cultivated land – such was the appearance of Simla at five miles' distance, and I naturally began to wonder where I should find the series of views for which I had undertaken this long journey. All the snow had not yet (March) disappeared from the top of Jakko, which is 8,000 feet above the sea, and on which the English love of pure air has induced them to build their houses, even to the very summit. A further acquaintance with Simla has not altogether banished the disappointment its first sight gave me, yet it is not to be condemned. It has afforded me a considerable number of pictures of a certain class, while, as regards the climate, nothing could be finer; and, were the scenery far inferior to what it is, one should still be satisfied and thankful to know that here one has escaped that frightful heat which this season has been laying man and beast prostrate in the plains. Its great defect to the photographer is its lack of water; I do not mean for the purpose of carrying on his manipulations, but for introducing into his views. There are no lakes, no rivers, and scarcely anything like a stream in this locality, neither is there a single object of architectural interest, no rustic bridges, and no ivy-clad ruins, trees, and mountains; and the beautiful play of light and shadow about them are, therefore, all that the photographer has to compose his picture. On some days we get a very good view of the higher and snowy ranges of the Himalayas, but they are too distant, and the atmosphere not sufficiently clear to render them in a photograph.

It was Bourne's skill in manipulating 'the beautiful play of light and shadow' that distinguishes so many of his photographs. He was captivated by the clear light he found in India.

In fact, the more brilliant the sunshine, the more I love to see the image on the ground glass; and, arriving just fresh from England, where the dampness and thickness of the atmosphere so sadly mar the brilliancy and crispness of the picture, and are so unfavourable for producing anything like breadth of effect, I have frequently stood transported at the wonderful brilliancy of the image portrayed on the screen, at the beautiful touches of sunlight amongst the trees, and the fine masses of broad light and shadow everywhere pervading the picture.

He was soon busy with his camera seeking out the picturesque in Simla: panoramic views of the town framed by imposing clumps of trees, the Mall snaking its way through the huddle of precariously perched buildings, the substantial houses of the more notable residents and the waterfall that gave him the only opportunity to include water in his compositions. He deplored the licence artists took in their paintings simply to present a pleasing effect. In one of a series of long letters to the *British Journal of Photography* he drew attention to recent sketches in the *Illustrated London News* of Peterhoff and Barnes Court.

We were amazed here to see how greatly the artist had *drawn* on his imagination, and pressed into his service beautiful overhanging trees, which, no doubt, ought to have been there, but were not. If you are in possession of, and will refer to the number [of the *Illustrated London News*] in April which contains it, and compare the view of Peterhoff with the accompanying photograph taken from the same spot, you will see how far we can rely on these artists' creations.

Bourne decided to explore the higher regions of the Himalayas when the onset of the rains shrouding the hills in mist prevented any serious photography in Simla. On 29 July 1863 he left Simla with a retinue of thirty porters carrying cameras, tents and provisions, returning ten weeks later with 147 negatives of some remarkable views, many photographed for the first time. The following year he penetrated as far as Kashmir and the account of his journey includes an inventory of his photographic equipment.

My photographic requisites consisted of a pyramidal tent ten feet high by ten feet square at the base, very simple in construction, having merely a bamboo rod at each end of the four corners, and opening and closing like an umbrella. [This served the purpose of a portable dark room.] . . . My stock of glass consisted of 250 plates, 12″ × 10″, and 400 plates, 8″ × 4½″. I had two boxes of chemicals divided into compartments, each bottle fitting into its own compartment – one box being a duplicate of the other – so that should one 'come to grief' down some precipitory mountain, I might have the other to fall back upon. Besides these I had my field box, and a 'khilta' full of stock or spare chemicals. My cameras, two in number, were of the square bellows form, very light and portable, fitted with Grubb's aplanatic and Dallmeyer's triplet lenses; the doublet and triplet singlets were not then out. One box contained my two mounted glass bottles, which were absurdly heavy, camera top, and sundry little loose articles. Another contained four Winchester quart bottles – two for both solutions, one for spirits of wine, and the other for distilled water. . . . In all my photographic requisites formed about twenty loads.

Notwithstanding an unfortunate accident when his porters dropped a box of eighty-four 12″ × 10″ glass plates from which he was able only to salvage about twelve or eighteen pieces for his 8″ × 4½″ camera, and also the loss of some of his negatives through crazing by damp, Bourne found conditions good for photography in Kashmir. He was especially pleased to find 'no dust to generate pinholes, seldom any wind to ruffle either the temper or the trees.' The high quality of his work impressed professional photographers back home in England.

How travelling through such sultry scenes, oppressed betimes with heat, wind and dust, Mr Bourne has managed to secure such faultless pictures we cannot imagine; for there is not a speck or spot to disfigure them, not a trace of fog, no fracture of the collodion even at the corners, no pinholes, and, in brief, none of those technical shortcomings so commonly met with in the productions of all save a few of our best home artists.

During his last Himalayan expedition in 1865–66, Bourne reached 18,600 feet in the Manirung Pass where he succeeded in taking three extremely good photographs before clouds came down and obscured the view. At that time no one equalled Bourne in recording the grandeur of mountains but he himself was not entirely satisfied with his work.

Peterhoff and Barnes Court. From *Illustrated London News*, 25 April 1863.

But while I yield to none in admiration of the finest productions of photography, I cannot help remarking (and those who have had large experience with the camera in mountainous countries will bear me out in the assertion) that it fails more or less in the rendering of distances and mountains – the former appearing much too hazy and indistinct, the latter unnaturally dwindled down and distant. This remark, of course, does not apply to mountains which are close to the camera.

To appreciate the extent of Bourne's technical skill one must know something of the difficulties besetting photography in the tropics in those early days. Bourne like many other photographers used the wet collodion process invented by F. S. Archer in 1850. This involved coating a glass plate with collodion (basically guncotton dissolved in ether and alcohol), sensitizing it in a bath of nitrate of silver solution and exposing it in the camera while it was still moist. It required considerable practice to coat the larger plates evenly (12″ × 16″ and 16″ × 20″) as the collodion could start to dry before the entire plate had been covered. Bourne also found that the rapid evaporation of the ether sometimes prevented the collodion flowing freely over the plate. Small particles of dust in the air would adhere to the wet plates disfiguring the subsequent negatives with 'pinholes' and spots. P. H. Egerton in his *Journal of a Tour through Spiti to the Frontier of Chinese Thibet* (1864) expressed the frustration experienced by many photographers.

Certainly photography in these remote regions is carried on under difficulties, for my collodion shrivels up and peels off the plate when drying, though carefully sheltered from the sun and wind; and I am constantly losing some of my best pictures in this way.

On top of all that the intense heat was capable of splitting flimsily-made cameras. Cameras constructed of well-seasoned wood, preferably mahogany, and bound in brass, were strongly recommended for use in India. In the rainy season it was not unusual for lenses, plates and paper to be covered with mildew, springs to rust and shutters to become sluggish.

The need to develop and fix the collodion plate immediately after exposure required the use of a mobile dark room (usually a tent) when the photographer was working in the field. The main drawback to the wet collodion process was the enormous amount of equipment needed at hand. Despite all these difficulties, however, some photographers still preferred using wet collodion in order to obtain finely detailed prints even when alternative dry plate processes became available.

Exposure time depended upon the subject and the weather. Large landscapes taken by the wet collodion process might require anything from thirty seconds to over a minute. A breeze which stirred the leaves in a tree could ruin a photograph. An article on 'Photography in India' in *Photographic News* stipulated that

the time which can be employed here for out-door work is very short; from half-past six to eight o'clock in the morning being about the extreme limits . . . Earlier than half-past six the shadows are long and dark, and fine negatives cannot be obtained; at half-past seven or eight, the wind almost invariably begins to blow, setting every leaf and branch in motion, and further landscape operations for the day are out of the question. Occasionally, there is a total absence of wind during the greater part of the day.

Samuel Bourne overcame these difficulties with such marked success that a contributor to the *British Journal of Photography* wished

to know something more concerning Mr Bourne's method of operating, for, when we examine some of the temples of white marble, and find the most perfect softness pervading their details, and in the same picture trees and general vegetation, together with figures, water and other surrounding subjects, all in correct keeping – no effect obtained at the expense or by the sacrifice of any other part – we are constrained to admit that the artist is possessed of manipulative or chemical resources shared in common by few, and a knowledge of which would be gladly received by our readers.

Another envious contributor remarked on the

clearness and cleanness of the skies [in Bourne's photographs]. None of them were blacked out, and all of them without spot or blemish of any kind. . . . Now after seven years' practice as a professional photographer, I cannot do this.

With such a talented photographer as partner the firm of Bourne and Shepherd could not fail to succeed. In 1866 it issued an impressive catalogue listing over 1500 views of India for sale. In 1870 Samuel Bourne returned to England and fifteen years later Charles Shepherd left, but the firm survived and for many years visitors to India continued to buy Bourne and Shepherd photographs to remind them of their travels in that country.

BOOK LIST

Aberigh-Mackay, G., *Twenty-One Days in India*, 1890.

Bourne, S., Series of articles on his photographic expeditions in the Himalayas, *British Journal of Photography*, 1863–70.

Bremner, C., *A Month in a Dandy*, 1896.

Buck, E., *Simla Past and Present*, 1904.

Carey, W., *Guide to Simla*, 1872.

Cumming, C. G., *In the Himalayas*, 1886.

Dalhousie, Lord, *Letters*, 1972.

The Delhi Sketch Book, 1850s.

Diver, M., *Honoria Lawrence*, 1936.

Dufferin, Lady, *Our Viceregal Life in India*, 1889.

Duncan, S. J., *The Simple Adventures of a Memsahib*, 1895.

Eden, E., *Up the Country*, 1866.

Hoffmeister, W., *Travels*, 1848.

Hyde, H., *Simla and the Hill States*, 1961.

Jacquemont, V., *Letters from India*, 1836.

Kincaid, D., *British Social Life in India*, 1938.

King, A., 'Hill Stations' (*Social Action*, 1976).

Kipling, R., *Kim*, 1901.

Lang, J., *Wanderings in India*, 1859.

Lytton, Lord, *Letters*, 1906.

Menzies, S., *Lord William Beresford*, 1917.

Princep, V., *Imperial India*, 1880.

Punjab Gazetteers, 1887–9.

Russell, W., *Diary in India*, 1860.

Surtees, V., *Lady Canning*, 1976.

Towelle's Guide to Simla, 1890.

Wilson, A., *The Abode of the Snow*, 1875.

UNPUBLISHED MANUSCRIPTS IN THE INDIA OFFICE RECORDS

Manuscript journal entitled 'The Log of a Griffin' by Edward Raleigh *MSS.Eur.D.786*.

Papers of Jane Maria Strachey, Strachey Collection *MSS.Eur.F.127*.

Photocopy of Jane Maria Strachey's diary dated 1863 and 1869 *Photo.Eur.58*.

Letters of Henry Oldfield *MSS.Eur.C.193*.

Papers of Honoria Lawrence, Henry Lawrence Collection *MSS.Eur.F.85*.

John Lawrence Collection *MSS.Eur.F.90*.

Papers of the 1st Earl of Lytton, Lytton Collection *MSS.Eur.E.218*.

Plates

Captain C. P. Kennedy's house at Simla, built in 1822. Both the first Governor-
General and the first Commander-in-Chief in India established their headquarters
there (J. Luard, *Views in India, Saint Helena and Car Nicobar* [1838?]).

Elysium Hill with Auckland House on its right flank where Emily Eden stayed with
her brother, the Governor-General (W. L. L. Scott, *Views in the Himalayas*, 1852).

View from Jakko. In the middle-distance is the tower of Christchurch under construction. The building flying a flag is Bentinck Castle, for some years the residence of the Commander-in-Chief in India (W. L. L. Scott, *Views in the Himalayas*, 1852).

The unfinished church and the bazaar extending up the hill slopes (W. L. L. Scott, *Views in the Himalayas*, 1852).

Combermere Bridge, built in 1828 by Lord Combermere, Commander-in-Chief in India, to connect Simla and Chota Simla. The house in the centre was Abbeville where some of the best subscription balls and masquerades were held (G. P. Thomas, *Simla*, 1846).

One of a number of old temples near Simla. The lady in the foreground is seated in a jampan (W. L. L. Scott, *Views in the Himalayas*, 1852).

Until the 1880s when reservoirs were built, Simla depended largely on local springs for water. In this lithograph by J. Luard, 'a Bhestie of Bengal having filled one mussock (skin) is filling another, while a native of Madras, not a regular water carrier, is waiting for an opportunity to fill a kedgeree pot . . . . The gentleman in the large hat and blue coat, is an officer in the Company's regiment of Goorkas, who resided at Simla in 1826.' (J. Luard, *Views in India, Saint Helena and Car Nicobar* [1838?]).

A general view of the ridge and bazaar, taken from 'Bonnie Moon', one of the oldest boarding houses in Simla and home of its first museum.

The Viceregal Lodge and Boileaugunge (i.e. West Simla) with the Snowy Range in
the distance. Naturally the peak that offered some of the best views in Simla was
carefully selected as an appropriate site for the Viceroy's residence.

The Mall. The half-timbered building looking vaguely like a Swiss chalet was the
General Post Office. In the foreground stands a chaprassie, with an official dispatch
box.

Arrival of the mail tonga at the General Post Office.

The General Post Office on the left of the Mall which leads to the Town Hall with Christchurch and thickly wooded Jakko just beyond. Lady Dufferin, in whose time the Town Hall was completed, likened it to a cathedral, but Lord Curzon described it as being 'a gaunt and graceless protuberance'.

The Mall below the Club. The principal road in any hill station was always known as the Mall; from it other roads branched and to it they eventually returned. It was the centre of fashion, gossip and intrigue.

A photograph by Samuel Bourne of part of the road around Jakko. 'Mount Jakko seems to be the pivot around which the Simla community revolve in their morning and evening perambulations. The circuit round this hill is about two or three miles, and . . . in the evening it forms the nucleus around which groups of ladies and gentlemen are observed to congregate.' (C. J. French, who was a member of Lord Auckland's entourage in 1838-9).

Simla in 1888. The wooden Tudor building high on the hill is the Telegraph Office. Below it are government offices. These clusters of official buildings 'made Simla monstrous' in Lady Curzon's view. Note the corrugated iron roofs.

The Lakkar Bazaar and the road to Tibet. Lady Reading wished she could visit 'the bazaars incognito . . . . In Simla it would have been utterly impossible because everything that happened there became common knowledge in club and bazaar at great speed, owing to the constriction of society dictated by the lie of the land. As you went along the Mall you were visible to the bazaars several hundred feet below you, just as movements below could be spied upon from above.' (I. Butler, *The Viceroy's Wife*, 1969).

The lower bazaar — 'the crowded rabbit-warren that climbs up from the valley to the Town Hall at an angle of forty-five. A man that knows his way there can defy all the police of India's summer capital; so cunningly does verandah communicate with verandah, alley-way with alley-way, and bolt-hole with bolt-hole.' (R. Kipling, *Kim*).

A photograph by Samuel Bourne of Simla during the winter of 1867/8. On the left is the Club facing the store of J. Anderson, wine-merchant and general dealer. The figures are Tibetan traders.

66

A photograph by Samuel Bourne of Simla in winter. 'And yet to see Simla in the winter time, its fanciful summer house dwellings covered with cleaving roofs of snow; the tall pines fretted over with icicles and frosted with snow drift on leaf and branch . . . and above all the everlasting snowy range shining out in its grandest aspect . . . is indeed worth while to essay a winter journey to the Himalayas.' (J. F. Wyman, *Calcutta to the snowy range, by an Old Indian*, 1865).

A photograph by Samuel Bourne of the 'Yarrows' and the surrounding hills taken
from 'Inverarm'. Lord Roberts, who spent many seasons at Simla, once exclaimed:
'At the best one gets very tired of the hills by the close of the summer.'

A distant view by Samuel Bourne of Peterhoff, which was the residence of the Viceroy from 1862 until the new Viceregal Lodge was built. It was said that more illustrious heads rested there at one time or another than in any other humble, five-bedroom house in the Empire.

Lord and Lady Canning with the Commander-in-Chief in India, Lord Clyde, 1860. Simla did not particularly appeal to Lady Canning, who wrote: 'I think the beauty of this place very questionable, it is such a sea of hill tops, and the snowy mountains are so far off, and the dryness makes all look wintry. . . . Here if one sees ten yards level one screams out "what a site for a house".'

A group of officials and relatives at Simla.
Standing: *first from left* Sir Henry Norman (Military Member of the Supreme Council in India); *fourth from left* Hon. Captain Alick Stewart; *fifth from left* Nina Plowden; *sixth from left* Allen Johnson (Military Secretariat); *seventh from left* Francis Norman (later Lieut.-General). Sitting: *first from left* Mrs Jane Maria Strachey; *third from left* Colonel Tombs; *fourth from left* Colonel Richard Strachey (later Lieut.-General).

The staff of the Foreign Department of the Government of India at Simla in 1870.
Included in the photograph are some of those Eurasian clerks and writers whose
social standing on the Simla scene was very insecure and lowly.

The Viceroy, Lord Northbrook, and his Executive Council in 1874, presumably outside Peterhoff. Under the Councils Act of 1861, the Executive Council included at least two members of the Civil Service, a military, legal and financial member, with the Commander-in-Chief of the Army as an extraordinary member. Lord Lawrence, the first Viceroy to move his Executive Council to Simla, is reported as saying: 'I believe we shall do more work here in one day than in five down in Calcutta.'

Barnes Court in 1882. Three years previously the house had been made the official residence of the Governor of the Punjab. It was a half-timbered building perched on a steep hill with commanding views to the south, east and west. Set in spacious gardens, probably no other house in Simla reproduced so convincingly the familiar landscape of an English country house.

Snowdon was made the official residence of the Commander-in-Chief in India from
1885. Lord Roberts and Viscount Kitchener were amongst its distinguished residents.

Everywhere paths led to small wooden bungalows with corrugated iron roofs perched
precariously on the sides of the hills.

A typical garden at Simla where English flowers, shrubs and trees flourished.

Melrose, 1886, the home of (General Sir) Ian Hamilton.

A rickshaw. Simla was a tangle of little roads, often too narrow for any vehicle bigger
than the rickshaw, which had replaced the jampan by the 1890s.

The Viceregal Lodge. An uncompromising English Renaissance style was chosen by its architects, Henry Irwin, the local Superintendent of Works and Captain H. H. Cole of the Royal Engineers. An unimpressed Secretary of State described it as being 'exactly like a Scotch hydro — the same sort of appearance, the same sort of architecture, the same sort of equipment of tennis lawns and sticky courts, and so forth. Inside it is comfortable, with suites of apartments comparable to those of the Carlton or the Ritz.'

The terrace gardens, Viceregal Lodge. Forty gardeners were employed when Lord Curzon lived there and another ten men were engaged to prevent the monkeys from damaging the plants. The stone terraces were constructed during Lord Minto's residence, 1905-10.

Viceregal Lodge. Lady Dufferin in her boudoir which was decorated in 'a bright
sort of brown', 1888.

Viceregal Lodge. Some of the furniture, such as this monstrous sideboard, was made
to conform with the Tudor architecture of the house.

Viceregal Lodge. The ballroom, heavy with Maple's lincrusta and paper ornamentation. But Lady Dufferin thought it a 'very fine room and outside the dancing space there is plenty of room for sitting as the wall is much broken up with pillars, leaving a sort of gallery round it.'

Viceregal Lodge. The gallery, which soared in a tremendous surge of elaborate wooden carvings to the full height of the house.

Lord and Lady Dufferin going to church in Simla in 1889.

The Viceroy's rickshaw coolies in their scarlet livery, 1885.

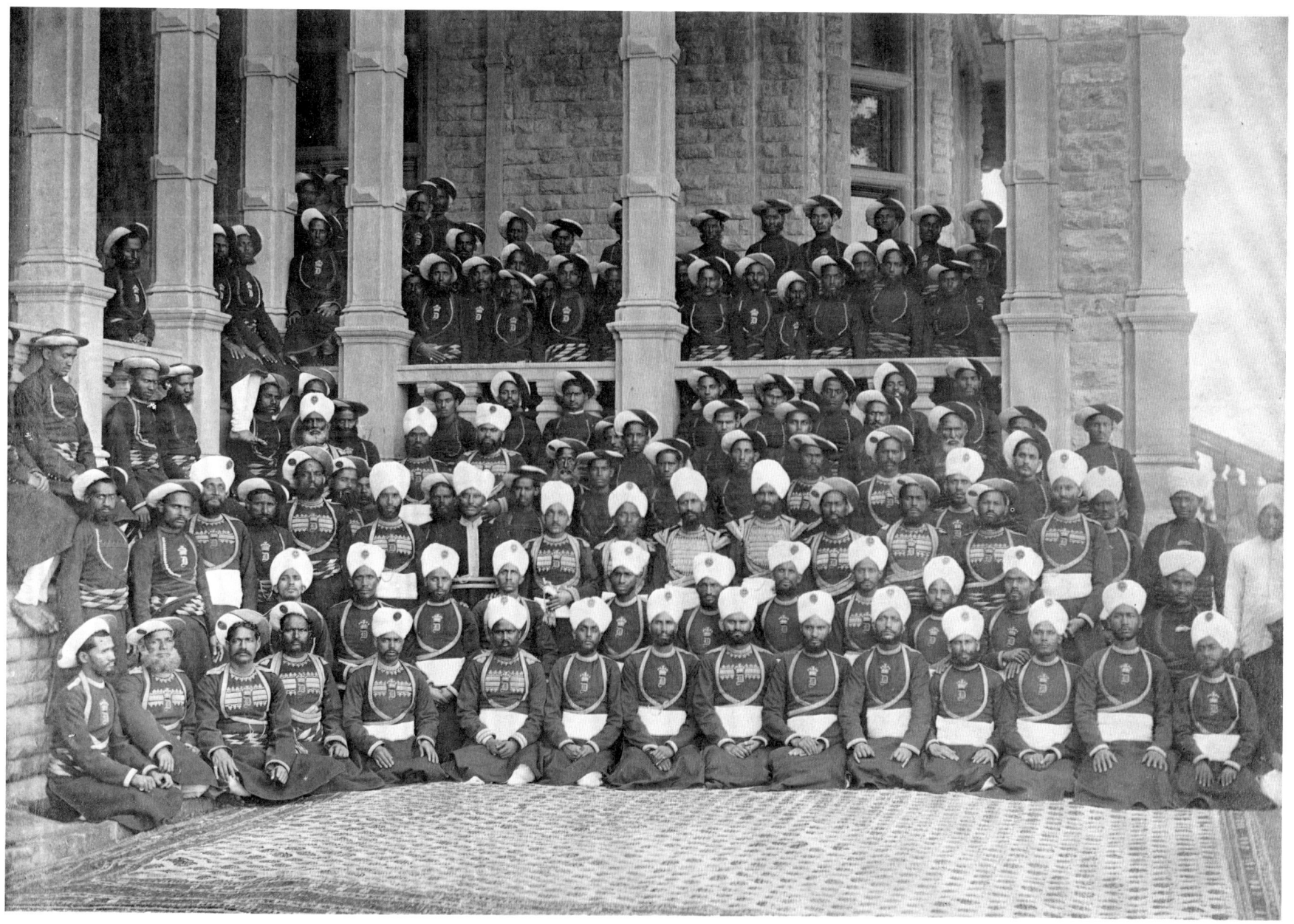

Viceregal Lodge servants, 1888.

Christchurch, built on a ridge over 7,000 feet above sea-level, is one of the most prominent landmarks in Simla. Although the foundation stone was laid in September 1844 it was thirteen years before the church was finished. The fresco surrounding its chancel window was designed by Lockwood Kipling, Rudyard's father. The adjacent terrace was a popular meeting place on Sunday mornings and the only suitably large and level space for parades.

A wedding party at Simla in 1875. 'It has always struck me that the bridegroom looks rather out of place at a wedding, . . . but nowhere does he appear more so than at a wedding in the Himalaya. The bride must of course return to her sedan, for, to say nothing of the sun, the dust would utterly spoil her dress were she to walk: so the bridegroom must perforce either walk or ride by her side, and most men would prefer the latter alternative, since it is not every one who can keep up gracefully with the pace of four shuffling sedan-bearers in the prime of condition.' (F. R. Chesney, *A True Reformer*, 1873).

Viceregal staff picnic in the nearby valley of Annandale in 1891.

The race-course at Annandale. With a descent of 70 feet in 200 yards, and a precipice immediately below, it must have ranked as one of the most hazardous courses in the world. Racing there was later made safer by enlarging the course and cutting into the side of the hill.

A performance of *The Mikado* at Simla in 1886. Eight or nine plays were usually staged by the Amateur Dramatic Club during the season. A Gilbert and Sullivan production at the local Gaiety Theatre was certain to fill the house.

Fancy dress in 1886, a vintage year for fancy balls at Simla.

The Hotel de Paris, a building with a chequered career: formerly the Simla Bank, then the New Club which, failing to compete with its rival, the United Service Club, closed down in 1891. It re-emerged as the Hotel de Paris and was later renamed the Grand Hotel.

Elysium Hotel on Elysium Hill.

Auckland House was the residence of Lord Auckland, the Governor-General. His sister, Emily Eden, who greatly enjoyed her brief stay at Simla, regretted leaving Auckland House. 'Poor dear house,' she wrote, 'I am sorry to see it despoiled, we have had seven as good months here as it is possible to pass in India: no trouble, no heat, and if the Himalayas were only a continuation of Primrose Hill, or Penge Common, I should have no objection to pass the rest of my life in them.' From being the home of Governors-General it became a boarding house, then a hotel until 1868, when a girls' school was established there.

A photograph by Samuel Bourne of one of the three European cemeteries in existence towards the end of the century. Among local notables buried in Simla were Herr F. Goldstein, bandmaster to His Excellency the Viceroy; the enterprising entrepreneur, Mr Barrett; Major Goad, formerly owner of Tally-Ho Hall, and Colonel Robert Tytler, founder of Simla's first museum and also a very competent photographer.

The small temple dedicated to Hanuman, the monkey god, on the top of Jakko. An old fakir looked after the troops of monkeys who lived there and descended on the town when the snows came. 'It was a wonderful sight, the spectacle of the monkeys in their thousands careering about the Mall, or seated on the rails or the rocks, in the early morning.' (A subaltern in a letter, 1862).

98

Native priests at Simla.

Photograph by J. C. Oman of Charles De Rusett, 1894. The son of C. W. De Rusett, general contractor and photographer at Simla, he rejected his European upbringing and for two years lived on Jakko as the disciple of the local fakir. On becoming a fakir himself, he donned a leopard skin and retreated to the seclusion of a temple near Annandale.

The Hindustan and the Tibet Road leading to Narkanda north-east of Simla. Work
on this road was begun at Kalka in 1850 in fulfilment of Lord Dalhousie's grand
design for good communications right up to the borders of Tibet.

A photograph by Samuel Bourne of the Priory, taken from Jakko with the Mahasu
Hills in the background. This was the residence of W. H. Russell during his period of
convalescence in Simla.

A photograph by Samuel Bourne of The Retreat at Mashobra about six miles from Simla. At one time the residence of Lord William Hay, the Commissioner of the Simla Hill States, it was frequently rented by the Commanders-in-Chief in India including Sir Frederick Roberts who found it a welcome 'refuge from the (sometimes) slightly trying gaiety of Simla.'

The Rana of Koti, head of one of the ruling families who possessed considerable land in the vicinity of Simla (J. Forbes Watson and J. W. Kaye, *The People of India*, 1869, vol. 4).

Watercolour by R. Clint. A hillman with a load on his back, Simla, 1866. The hillmen often used to carry wide planks of wood from the forest interiors into Simla. If they met a person on horseback, they were expected to scramble out of the way.

Watercolour by R. Clint. A hillwoman smoking, Simla, 1866.

The Sipi Fair, held in a small valley about six miles from Simla. This two-day event
every May was eagerly awaited by the villagers of the neighbouring hills and
recognised by the local authority as a public holiday.

A viaduct on the Kalka-Simla railway. Until November 1903 the railway terminated at Kalka and the remaining sixty miles to Simla were covered in a tonga in about eight hours. Passengers travelling by tonga were advised by Murray's *Handbook of India* to 'wear close fitting spectacles or veils as a protection against injury to the eyes from particles of stone or metalling.'

The train approaching Simla. Journey's end was appreciated by all those travellers who had endured an uncomfortable ride in a train that swayed alarmingly on its 2′6″ gauge lines.

A photograph by Samuel Bourne looking towards Christchurch from Jakko.